FAMILY CAMPING

All the family enjoy camping in the countryside. Photo: Eurocamp

FAMILY CAMPING

by

Barbara Bignell

CICERONE PRESS
MILNTHORPE, CUMBRIA

ISBN 1 85284 176 1
© Barbara Bignell 1995

Dedication

To Julie, Jonathan, Sue and Richard, who in addition to taking exams and following their own careers have erected tents, made tea, cooked meals and if deadlines have been close, generally kept the author functioning - and after the nail breaking work is over they still manage to smile for the camera. Thanks team.

Front Cover : *Top -* Camping in the French Pyrenees.
Bottom - Family Camping with Canvas Holidays.
Photographs by Canvas Holidays

Contents

ADVICE TO READERS

Readers should note that this book is a general guide to camping and the outdoor life. Every effort has been made to ensure accuracy but Barbara Bignell and Cicerone Press cannot be held responsible for any consequences that may arise from errors and omissions.

All information has been checked as far as possible and the contents are believed to be correct at the time of going to press. Changes to materials and designs are occurring all the time. Recommendations only apply to the specific item covered and not every piece of equipment mentioned has been tested. There can be dangers associated with camping and outdoor pursuits and when taking part, all safety precautions should be followed.

Acknowledgements

Many companies, Tourist Boards and their personnel have helped with my work, not just for this book but over the years. They have provided information, tents and equipment for testing, a pitch on their campsite, sometimes a photograph to accompany a feature. To all my contacts I say 'very many thanks' for your assistance and in particular:

Valerie Back for walking out Norfolk coastal routes and inspecting umpteen toilet blocks, Paul Bibby (Peter Storm), David and Melanie Bridle (*Caravan, Motorcaravan and Camping Mart* magazine), The Camping and Caravanning Club - Peter Frost, Erica Anderson, Janet Edwards and Debbie Moss; Denise Dawson (Canvas Holidays), The Caravan Club, The Camping and Outdoor Leisure Association, Coleman UK Plc, Craghoppers Ltd, Clive Edwards (Alan Rogers Site Guides), Eurocamp, Wendy Fellingham (Ordnance Survey), Carlos Fernandez (Marechal, France), John and Margaret Fieldhouse (Cabanon), Fiona Gordon (First Public Relations), Mr Griffiths of Sawtry, Headwater Holidays, Becky Hughes (Karrimor), Merrell Footwear, HF Holidays, Grangers (proofing products), Jane Jones (Isle of Wight Tourist Office), Mountain Equipment, Philip Pond, Bryan Pool (Marechal UK), Ramblers Holidays, Relum Ltd, Risol Ltd, Rohan Designs plc, Mr and Mrs Salt of Great Gransden, David Smith (Lichfield tents), Ted and Pat Stocker and Wendy Fairman for getting us interested in camping in the first place. Sue and Richard Phillpott for erecting scores of frame tents, Julie Johnston for checking this manuscript and her husband Jonathan for his tolerance.

All photographs are by the author apart from the following to whom we are very grateful:

Camping in the Loir Valley - yes, the one without the 'e'!

INTRODUCTION
Why camp and which type of camping?

There are many reasons why people take to the great outdoors in a tent. The one most quoted is FREEDOM but there's a lot more to this addictive pastime. Just think, after quite a small outlay it is possible to wake up in a grassy meadow with a trickling brook at your front door. Turn round and there are rugged peaks as a backcloth.

Of course, you may go for the sound of waves or the hot sun to coax you out of your sleeping bag. Then there are visits to historical centres, York, Chester, Venice, Rome, you name it. There are so many possibilities once you've bought the tent and equipment.

And we're not talking about just one annual holiday. There can be many a school holiday and weekend spent in the fresh air. The camping venue may take in a beach to examine the rock pools or maybe there will be visits to theme parks for a few white knuckle rides and the thousand and one other attractions around the country.

There are families perhaps with several children who find that without their camping trips the bank balance wouldn't stretch to a holiday at all. There's no need to splash out on all the gear to begin with. Raid the kitchen cutlery drawer and cupboards - and most people already own or can beg or borrow sleeping bags or duvets as well as picnic chairs.

True, the time will come when you'll want to buy a separate set of gear but that can be left until you discover exactly what is needed. Walkers, climbers, cyclists, cavers and water sports enthusiasts may just want a simple unit to use overnight. We won't be covering specialist tents fit for Everest but if members of the party want to take off with a mountain bike, hang glider or a kayak they may still prefer to use a family type model with lots of height and elbow room.

Some folk enjoy the solitude of a small camping site with little more than a water tap and toilet. Others look for a swimming pool, disco and restaurant - and 90,000 or more join a club. They might buy a quality frame tent and all the mod cons available - I've even seen carpet in a frame tent - and enjoy the company of other campers to the full. The tent can be an affordable country retreat, a real 'home from home'. If everyone in the family is going to enjoy the experience as much comfort as possible should be provided.

Because of the great diversity of outdoor interests, the tent you pick does need to be the right style for the job. Will you be staying on one site for two weeks or moving on every day or two? Today's camping is all about choice. Don't be lured into buying the first frame tent you fall in love with - as with marriage the hasty step could be repented at leisure.

Why not 'go lightweight' if you're touring or looking for a budget priced holiday? Look for the full height domes and chalets in nylon or polyester. There's no need to crawl about bent over like the top of a tent peg these days. Much will depend on the age of your children, of course. With disposable nappies and so many 'take-away' meals available, plus breakfast cereals and snacks that can be made with one boiled kettle, it's possible to use the tent for just bed and breakfast - perhaps a single burner stove could cope.

First-time campers may like the idea of a ready erected tent with all the equipment, including a refrigerator, ready and waiting on the campsite of their choice. At one time this 'instant camping' was only available on the continent but a few campsites in England and Ireland are offering tents ready for occupation. Read the advertisements in specialist magazines, study the brochures. Things change from year to year.

Setting up a lightweight camp

You may have already been on a ready-erected tent holiday and become hooked on the outdoor life. The time has come to buy your own unit ready for a weekend away when the sun shines. Are you wondering whether to buy a traditional frame tent or not - in cotton or lightweight nylon or polyester?

Of course, if you can sling the kids, dogs, partner and all the trappings into the car and just drive off you probably don't need this book. However if you are keen for the holiday or weekend trip to go as smoothly as a well oiled engine then a certain amount of planning and organization is advisable.

Some campers write several lists, others go as far as collating lists of lists. The lucky ones are really relaxed, they jot down a few notes which the family pet promptly chews up and they still come out smiling. You'll learn a lot by experience, it's true, but that can be expensive - for instance we quickly found that a 5 gallon water carrier took up too much room and was extremely heavy when full. One or two 1 gallon containers make water fetching a much more flexible affair. Children can help or, for those with more muscle, a gallon in each hand can be carried.

The purpose of this book is to point out a few short cuts. There's no mystery about camping, after all it's only everyday living, under canvas out of doors. However it can be a great family adventure with kids and parents loving almost every second.

Thinking back to 25 years ago when our two daughters and myself first agreed to dad's brainwave of 'Let's go Camping' still gives me goosebumps of pleasure. After just three weeks of owning our frame tent and one trial run we went off to Switzerland. 'If we don't like it' we said, 'We can always sell the lot and will still have had a holiday abroad at a lot less than a brochure package.'

The fact that I am still camping - in a high dome these days, when I'm not testing other models - and writing about my experiences must be some kind of recommendation. Do your homework and then 'Go for it'.

CHAPTER ONE

Choosing a frame tent

MATERIALS

For family camping the traditional cotton frame tent is probably the most stable and more comfortable of the 'portable homes'. It has a healthier feel about it and will please the cook and child minder when he/she wants space for a baby's cot and elbow room to wield the potato masher. There are some good roof lockers and luggage trailers about, which means you do have the option of packing all mod cons including the kitchen washbasin.

The largest frame tents such as a Lichfield Almeria 6 berth is a grand 16ft 6in by 15ft with a height of 7ft 7in. It is transported in 3 kitbags weighing a total of 116lbs. If you insist on a frame tent design in the lighter nylon fabric look around, there aren't many in the latest brochures but they do exist. You may be asking 'but what difference is there between man-made materials and cotton?' Let me explain.

Cabanon Elody frame tent in cotton

As far as the general feel goes, think of shirts or tops. Do you prefer cotton or polyester? Synthetics can be sweaty. Tents made of nylon or polyester can attract water droplets on the inside in certain weather conditions. If you don't touch the roof all is usually well but if your arm strays upwards you could get an unscheduled shower bath. I will quickly add that this is usually nothing too drastic, more of a sprinkle. In the main the advantages of synthetics outweigh the downside: besides being light in weight and folding up quite small, nylon and polyester dry quicker than cotton. Providing plenty of ventilation will help to keep condensation at bay.

You'll soon find that camping is all about compromise and priorities. If we could tuck the largest frame tent, a full size table and chairs, 3 tier kitchen unit with side washing-up bowl, plus a portaloo with separate tent and all the other gear into the smallest car or rucksack there would be much rejoicing. But we can't and that is where it's a matter of decisions, decisions.

This could also be the reason for the popularity of ready-erected tent holidays. But even this seemingly perfect mode of camping has its drawbacks. One of them being that if you can't take advantage of the generous amount of off-season budget packages, ready-erected tents can be expensive. The idea of buying your own tent and gear might suddenly become very attractive.

A good quality cotton tent from one of the well-known names such as Cabanon, Marechal or Lichfield could last for several generations. Our Danish-made OBI, a make which doesn't seem to be available at present, was bought 20 years ago. It is still used today by Julie, our eldest daughter, and her husband Jonathan and/or a group of work colleagues and still has plenty of years left. (Before readers get out the biros OBI caravan annexes are still going strong.)

Correct storage is very important though. Don't come back from a camping trip with the tent in a damp state, throw it in the garden shed and expect it to be in good condition when you next need it. Once the dreaded mould takes hold it eats away like rust on a car. It smells too. If you are unlucky enough to find a patch of black or dark spots of mould before the material has taken on the appearance of a colander, there are products to stop the rot. A weak solution of 5 volume peroxide bleach is one but take care, it's safer to buy the proper cleaner from a camping shop. (See Chapter Fourteen - re-proofing a tent.) Although the rot may be halted those little black spots are almost impossible to remove.

Prevention is best. Dry the tent off thoroughly after each trip, erect and peg fully if possible to prevent shrinkage, or rather to keep the tent in shape. Make sure all the double thick rubbing strips on roof and around zips are as dry as the proverbial desert and then store in a dry, not hot place. Beware of the double thickness of material along the inside of the ridge on some nylon tents. The idea is excellent but this inside ridge strip, the length that actually comes into contact with the poles, may be made of cotton which will take longer to dry than nylon.

Some manufacturers are now advising campers to grease the poles before storing away for the winter. In any case keep metal poles away from the canvas; iron-mould is more or less impossible to remove.

If you can't re-erect the tent in the garden, as a last resort it may have to be left on the spare bedroom chairs or floor or perhaps over the banisters to be turned over and around every few hours. My nylon tent drapes well over the rotary clothes drier in the garden. First of all any mud on the lower section (or mudflap if it's a chalet or frame type) is washed off then over the drier it goes, to be turned occasionally like a giant mushroom in a pan.

It has been said many times that nylon can be packed away wet. A day or so may not hurt but are you old enough to remember plastic macs and the smell of one that had been folded up wet for days? Enough said. Treat

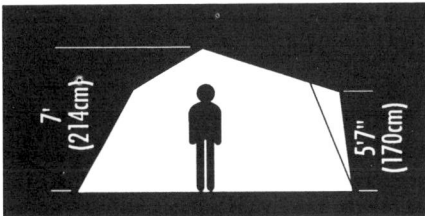

Dimensions and weight of a Lichfield Montana 4 with two separate inners and a rear door (see opposite p17 for a picture of this tent)

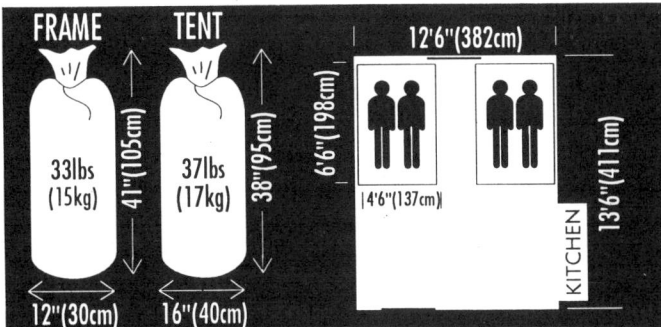

TOTAL WEIGHT 70lbs(32kg)

13

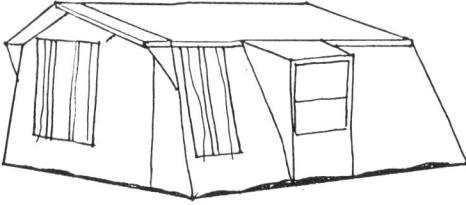

Chateau 6 frame tent. three separate inners across the rear wall

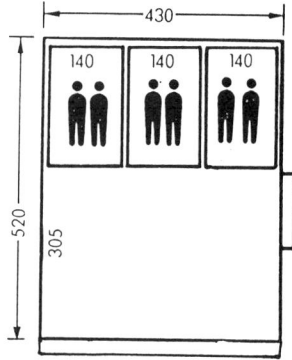

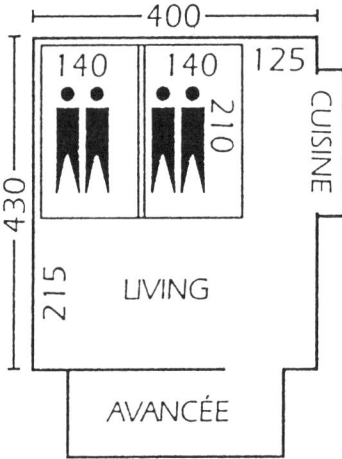

Cabanon Luxor 4 with L-shaped lliving area

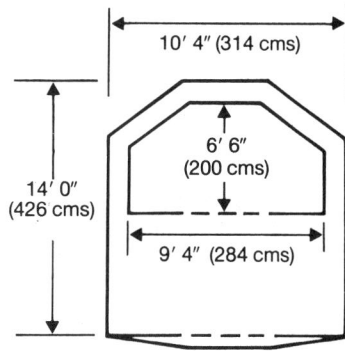

Pyramid layout of a Relum Izmir (see opposite p16 for a picture of this tent)

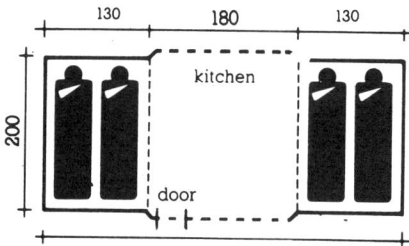

VIS-A-VIS P 954   440
Legs: 4
Height: 205
Weight: 60 lbs
Bags: 2

Cabanon Vis-a-Vis

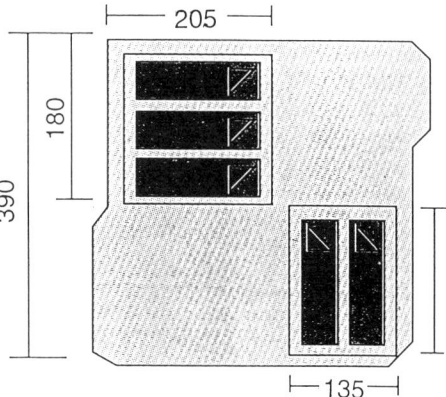

Raclet Iris with two separate inners

14

Transport should be considered

all tents kindly and they will give good service.

DESIGNS - WHICH SIZE, WHICH TYPE?

Look through any frame tent catalogue and you'll see models that look much the same. You may even pick out the prettiest/ most environmentally friendly colour, the most reasonably priced and then write out the cheque. True, it might sound as though that 2,3,4, 5 or 6 berth was just made for your particular family. But wait, a bit of a questionnaire is needed here. How old are your children, is your planned family complete yet? A toddler can soon become a teenager with legs like a giraffe and a range of holiday gear that wouldn't look lost in a motorway coach. Is that neat little 3 berth going to cope?

On the other hand, can your existing vehicle deal with anything larger? There are roof top luggage carriers and trailers which make transportation easier. You may decide that it's worth spending the extra so that you can take your own loo and toilet tent, your family size barbecue and so on. Check the weight your car roof can safely take and store light gear such as chairs up aloft.

Let's divide the frame tent into sections. 1. Frame 2. Dimensions. 3. Inner tent and number of bedrooms. 4. Living space and kitchen. 5. Windows and door/s, wardrobe rail, canopies, roll-up front wall etc.

1. **Frame.** At one time it would be have been difficult to find a large family tent with anything but steel polework. Then alloy or dural frames began to filter in but at quite high prices. Today the costs seem to have evened out and there's sometimes a choice between steel and alloy, both types of frame using the same outer canvas. Raclet is one manufacturer that springs to mind.

15

Aluminium is lighter in weight but will it stand up to blustery weather as well as steel? On a well sheltered pitch, as can be found on most campsites used by families, there shouldn't be any problem but don't underestimate the strength of the wind. If you do like the idea of an alloy frame make sure it has steel corner pieces. This gives that extra strength where it may be needed.

Most frames are fitted with spring-linking, a great help at assembly stage when deciding which pole goes where. Some manufacturers, such as Lichfield, on selected models use a spring clip to keep legs attached to corner pieces. We have tested a frame tent without linking of any kind which left us feeling like participants in a game show. As fast as we connected leg to corner and started on another the first one fell out! Not a very common problem but it can happen. So insist on at least some kind of linking.

Cabanon tends to link the poles at every opportunity. Some of its roof frames are in just three main pieces. A jumble when you take them out of their bag or valise but they almost spring together on their own. Push button adjusters are another feature on some frames. A good idea if the ground is very uneven and you want to get a smooth line to the tent. Don't forget to read the erecting instructions. Some makers state that the tent should first be erected to the smallest size and some state the largest.

2. **Overall dimensions.** The bigger the better. Buy as much 'space' as you can afford, transport, store and generally manage. If you want to use a full size table and chairs, then get out the tape measure on the living area. Don't be misled by floor plans. If possible go for at least a 3 berth for two people, a 4 berth for three, a 5 berth for four and so on. This extra space will be appreciated in both the inner compartment and the living area.

Those little diagrams with bodies lined up like soldiers on parade may be fine in theory. Most allow 18-24in for each person, which is reasonable but have you ever tried to get dressed on a water bed? True, it's easy enough to step out of the inner or to pull on trousers while lying down but extra space at the side of the bed can be a boon even if it's only to put the alarm clock to save missing the ferry.

There's nothing wrong with manufacturers using the same size outer for a 4 and a 6 berth tent but its a point buyers should know about. A good example is the Lichfield Montana (see opposite p17 for a picture of this tent), a medium size family model. This measures 12ft 6in by 13ft 6in and can be bought as a 4 and a 6 berth. The former has two separate bedrooms and a corridor between the two leading to a rear door. As a 6 berth the

Montana has a sleeping compartment stretching right across the back wall. In both cases the length of the bed space is 6ft 6in and the kitchen and living areas stay the same.

Height of the outer can be more important than you realise. An inch or two either way can make a lot of difference to the comfort of day to day living as well as when erecting the tent. If, like ours, your family is on the tall side you can deal easily with say the 7ft 7in maximum height of a Relum Texas Ranch or a Lichfield Almeria. Not that this should be a barrier to campers who are of more general proportions. Just make sure you remember to clip inners to the frame before raising the tent to full height. (See Chapter Tree erecting a frame tent.)

However, the question has to be asked 'why cart around the extra canvas and weight needed if you feel happy with a maximum height of 6ft?' The price too is usually less. When working out the cash aspect remember that every zip, every inch of canvas or pole as well as every frill and flounce and the stitcher's effort will cost. Go for a basic tent if you want to save money. When it comes to looks only you can be the judge.

The pyramid shape as made by Cabanon, Lichfield and Relum is interesting (see opposite p16 for a picture of the Relum Izmir Pyramid tent). What you lose on the polework you gain on the canvas. Basically the tent is made up from a small number of poles assembled into two or three elongated arches (there must be an architectural term for this shape) or with a central pyramid pole. The canvas is positioned face down, the poles inserted and the canvas raised and pegged out at numerous points. There's a lot of canvas in a pyramid tent but it's a good looking, eye-catching design that is often the talk of the campsite.

Colour schemes over the years have gone from the downright outrageous to ditchwater dull. With more and more well screened pitches do we have to wake up to camouflage colours? I think not. Do the cheerful colours of windsurfing sails take away the attraction of a lake? Again a choice is to be found in most catalogues.

3. **Inner tent and bedrooms.** The basic sleeping compartment is just one tent. It may have two or three bedrooms divided by a roll-up, roll-down or in some cases roll sideways curtain. If you like to have your children within arms distance fair enough. Separate bedrooms do give that extra bit of privacy. A hanging wardrobe space between the two is even better. Going even further some models such as the Raclet Residence come in an L shape with a bedroom at the top and the second along and to one side, probably as far apart as it is possible to be without using two tents!

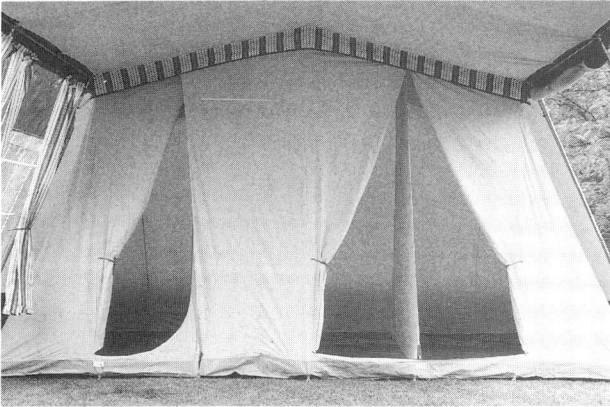

6 berth with two separate inners, one with a dividing curtain - and a hanging wardrobe between the two

Another family style to be considered is the vis-à-vis either in cotton or nylon. Nearly all the major manufacturers have at least one in their range. The vis-à-vis has one sleeping compartment at each side of a living area. The central lounge is full height and poles are fitted together frame style. The bedrooms can be ridge or dome shape but remember that the height will taper off. If you like to sit up in bed in the mornings to drink your tea or coffee watch this aspect. (More in Chapter Two - touring tents.)

Raclet Garance cotton vis-à-vis with framed kitchen at rear

Materials and ventilators of inner tents are important. Poly lighter in weight than 100% cotton. Most inners these days seer the former or a synthetic fabric of some kind. For maximum com should be at least one ventilator but if the weave is fairly open and you ʀ looking at a budget tent the vent may be dispensed with.

Perhaps of more importance is the tray type groundsheet. Make sure this has a good depth of at least 3in, though 4 or 5in are better. First of all it is designed to keep out the creepy crawlies that were enough to put most of us off the great outdoors in the old days. Secondly if you do get a good downpour of rain and the pitch is not well drained you don't want the water to reach the polycotton walls. If the sides and back soak up moisture this can be transferred to air beds and bedding resulting in an uncomfortable night - or nights if they don't have a chance to dry out. (More in Chapter Two - touring tents.) Bear in mind that a deep groundsheet tray can be easier to trip over as you enter the inner - we're back to that compromise again.

Some groundsheets are fitted with a generous amount of pegging points, others can be quite sparsely equipped. Most are welded and as long as the workmanship looks good there shouldn't be any problems. You'll need also to examine the quality of roof clips and the rubber rings and tapes that attach inner to frame. Most companies use a similar method and as long as the tape is well sewn to the inner it's possible to buy clips and rings separately, so don't dismiss the whole tent because you don't like metal clips or can't stand nylon.

Doorways or entrances to the inner might need to be considered. In sleeping compartments with divided bedrooms you may be provided with two or three zipped doorways. If you don't want youngsters wandering about without your knowledge stick to as few as possible. If you'd rather they didn't clamber over the air beds to get out, take all the doors you can get.

When choosing a tent, if the inner doorways of models on display are cordoned off ask for these to be removed. Take your shoes off before stepping inside and don't let the youngsters run wild. You need to try out the doorway types and zips. Some are a single curve, others are L shaped, many are made up from three zips, two horizontal and one vertical. If the entranceway is 'tight' you'll lose some of the comfort that frame tents are all about.

To complete the luxury there are usually one or two pockets stitched to the inner. These are useful for small objects but in 25 plus years of camping _'ve never used one.

4. **Living space and kitchen**. As mentioned the living area needs to be measured up for tables and chairs. Have you ever moved your lounge suite around at home and found that the doors, heaters etc. make certain lay-outs impossible? Then you'll begin to get the picture. You may prefer an L shape living area which I liked, especially when the children were quite small. The cooker could be sectioned off.

One point against this lay-out now that everyone is more safety conscious is that the little corridor often has a door in the back wall - plus a note saying that the exit must be kept clear. Rear doors are a good idea in one way but with this particular lay-out we've seen a frame tent go up in flames when a through-draught caused cooker flames to touch a side wall. Tents are inflammable and thought must always be given to this aspect - but don't get too paranoid.

There used to be a tent with a very handy canopy positioned in one side wall. The front wall could also be unzipped and rolled up. The problem was the kitchen window panel which came between the two. With side and front open at the same time the kitchen unit would have been left standing in a very vulnerable position. Children just love to run in one door and out of another. Even if there was no cooker alight, neither children nor kitchen unit would appreciate a collision.

Next, do you need a push-out (or inset) kitchen annex (see opposite p33). There's nothing wrong with a straight down kitchen window panel being fitted into one wall but you won't get the extra headroom of the push-out variety. On the other hand a kitchen annexe does need extra polework. This model will probably cost more and some campers may not need the luxury or be keen on the extra effort involved.

To give an instance the Relum Canaria range comes in a 3, 4 and 5 berth as does the Canaria K (the K stands for kitchen). Same tent, same dimensions but the K gives the cook some extra headroom.

Most kitchen panels are fitted with a mesh ventilator at the top and a translucent pvc window on the lower section. A pvc weatherflap on the outside can either be rolled up and held in place by tapes or rubber rings or battened down in a closed position by a variety of zips, tapes and toggles. The more expensive models will boast a smart zip at each side, budget designs may have cords and toggles. Both do the job although the zips should be more draught-proof.

Certainly a ventilator is a good feature and the cook will need as much daylight as possible. One of the latest Raclet models also has a pvc skylight in the roof, great stuff for a true 'holiday home' but remember - pick the design to suit your requirements. If you don't intend to cook full meals is a kitchen really necessary in the first place - again the option is there.

5. Doors, windows, canopies, roll-up front wall, pvc skirt and mudflap. All frame tents of course are fitted with at least one door. The zip is usually of the curved variety although the Relum Bungalow, and possibly others, use a single vertical type. The rear door in the main will only be found in more expensive models (see kitchen). Height of the doorway varies between about 5ft 6in and over 6ft and some have two sets of zips which means you can open up the top in 'stable door' fashion. This gives extra ventilation and at the same time keeps animals or children in or out as the case may be.

Stable door effect

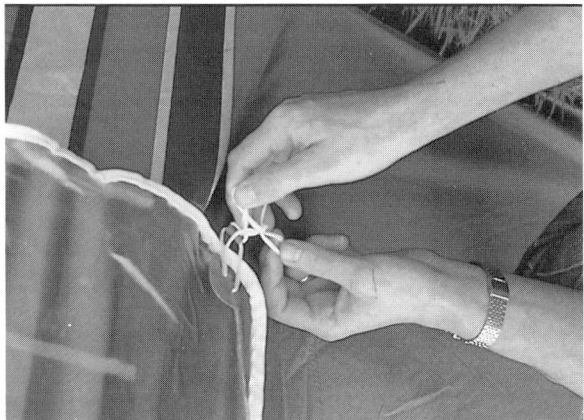

Cords cost less than zips

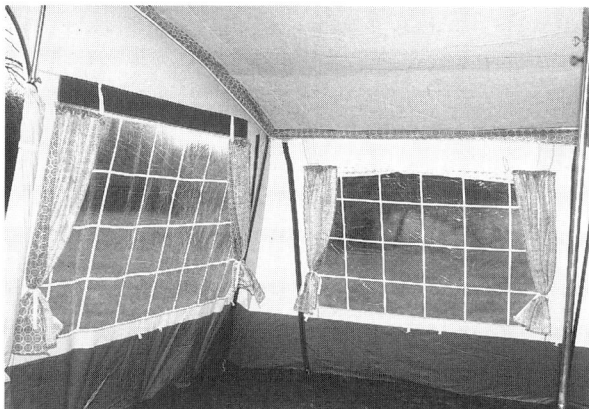

Georgian stlye windows
and roof liner

The quality of zips used on 'up-market' models will easily be detected, but it's not just zips. In the main, as with any other commodity, we do 'get what we pay for'. Cash may be saved in quality, but never fear, it could be just a lack of pretty looks.

Most frame tents will have one window which might be lattice or Georgian marked such as the Lichfield Valencia 4 or it could be of the kitchen variety as in the Valencia 4 de luxe. The Lichfield Almeria, the Raclet Tropic, the Cabanon Espace and the Marechal Pallas are given a whole range of panels containing pvc panes. Tents between these two examples might have two. It goes without saying that especially on dull days the more light available the better. Whether you go for the lattice type is up to you. Some manufacturers and campers can't do without them and they do seem to add to a tent's stylish appearance.

Our family's first ever window was far from attractive. We were into budget prices and the tent was a windowless Invader made by a firm in Coulsden. This was just as the French imports were starting to boast a window or two. Friends Pat and Ted Stocker who had introduced us to camping had added a window to their tent - why shouldn't we?

Not being a seamstress of any kind except the hopeless, I sat back one Sunday afternoon while my then husband and Pat crawled around the sitting room floor in an effort to give our family more light. We soon learned it is possible to stitch tent canvas on an ordinary sewing machine fitted with a heavier than usual needle. A mesh ventilator was stitched in as well as a rather basic canvas roll-down overflap.

The most nail-biting part is when the first cut in the canvas of your new tent is made. If I remember rightly the window was sewn in first, then the scissors were taken to the canvas. The reason for this little aside is to point out that anyone who can sew and has an old Singer (I know nothing about modern electric models) can deal with tent canvas - just have a few spare needles in case of breakage.

Curtains are usually provided although they are an optional extra on the Lichfield Challenger XL5 (see touring tents). On certain budget models such as a selection in the Czechoslovakian Relum catalogue curtains may be held in place by fairly basic methods. Others could have aluminium curtain rods. Again, the Relum way works well enough and you don't have the fiddle of threading rails through the top curtain hem. Some of these little comfort extras may not have the more refined appearance of others but does this matter if you are saving cash?

In luxury frame tents there will be at least one roll-up side canopy. This can usually be held out by poles or just unzipped and rolled up to be held in place by tapes. A roll-up (or to one side) front wall is also available. These two options mean that not only can you open right up to stop the family from melting in hot weather but they are also a good idea for spreading out the table and chairs.

To finish off the frame tent luxury you might be offered a roof liner which is good for looks as well as a certain amount of insulation. Then there's a kitchen divider but be very careful here and mind it doesn't catch alight. Some tents are fitted with a zip-out front section that has two positions, one giving a large lounge, the other a large enclosed porch.

As mentioned a wardrobe rail is useful. This is to be found between two separate bedrooms. In fact if you open up a new tent and can't make out what that slim pole and length of cord could be for it's the wardrobe. The options are many.

On the more practical side a lower skirt made of pvc material on the outer canvas can be useful. It's more easily sponged than cotton. Don't confuse a skirt with the 9in or so of mudflap or draught excluder usually provided. This might be positioned inside or outside the main canvas. It doesn't seem to matter which although inside does give a neater look.

Lichfield offer a range of pvc fire retardent kitchens and while talking about this West Midlands based company - John James Hawley - we can't stress enough that this is the only frame tent maker left in Britain. If you want to fly the flag buy a Lichfield.

HOW AND WHERE TO BUY

And now, as they say, a few words on the Hows and Wheres of choosing a new frame tent. Most of your questions should be answered in this book but it's a good idea to buy one or all of the specialist magazines. - *Camping, Outdoor, Caravan, Motorcaravan and Camping Mart* - or/and join The Camping and Caravanning Club, the only major club for tent campers. The Club publishes a monthly magazine (see Chapter Eleven). And I'm not just saying that because I write for them. This is my 25th year of Membership.

You'll find lots of information and addresses in these publications and the advertisements are good because that is where the news of exhibitions can be discovered. Many tents are bought at shows and exhibitions around the country. You may be lucky and find a bargain. 'Special exhibition' prices are to be seen at most of the venues, but make sure you aren't seduced by a colour scheme, a sunny day, and/or a youngster who says 'oh go on, dad or mum'.

Not that I'm against exhibitions. We still don't have enough of them, unfortunately. 'Campex' which is run by the Scout Shops takes place at three or four different locations during the month of May. You can actually go along and decide on the spot. Another great thing about 'Campex' is that entrance and car parking are free. In addition to the tent and trailer tent displays there are marquees with a whole range of cookers, sleeping bags, camping furniture, jackets, boots, in fact anything you're likely to need for a camping trip. (For up-to-the-minute information on dates and venues of 'Campex' see address and telephone number in appendix. Other exhibitions take place at Manchester G-Mex and the NEC Birmingham.)

If it's a trailer tent you're looking for the 'Caravan Show' at Earls Court might be a good place to go. The problem with these ideas is that the exhibitions only take place once a year so where do you go between times?

Look in your local paper. There may well be exhibitions in your area. In a farmer's meadow, at a garden centre, and of course at camping centres. In fact your local camping centre, whether it be a shop or part of a garden establishment' is probably one of the best places to find out about tents and camping equipment. You can see a whole range of goods, walk in and out of tents to your heart's content and generally get the feel of products available.

As with exhibitions, there aren't nearly enough camping centres but if the newspaper draws a blank look in the telephone *Yellow Pages*. This handy publication usually covers quite a wide area and you'll find addresses under - what else - 'Camping Equipment'. If you've decided to buy a particular make, perhaps because it's been recommended or you've seen a test report in a magazine, give the centre a ring first. Not all outlets stock every brand name. Some manufacturers will only allow one store to sell their product within a certain radius. A ring could save on the petrol bill.

How you will pay for the tent is perhaps the most important question. As with most other shops of the '90s it's usually possible to use any of the known methods: cash, cheque or credit card.

CHAPTER TWO

Lightweight and touring tents

Use the term Lightweight Camping and many people immediately think of backpacking. "What, cart everything including the kitchen sink on our backs, not likely." True, some folk take the lightweight bit to extremes and it can be quite a stimulating challenge to get house and home into one rucksack. I've heard of backpackers going as far as cutting an inch or two from the handle of a toothbrush to get the weight down.

However, that style of camping is not covered in this book. Our aim is to help families choose the right gear for their particular type of camping - putting the emphasis on as much comfort as possible.

We're talking in this chapter about lowish level, fairly sheltered camping during the summer months. The tents are relatively light in weight and a minimum amount of equipment would be taken. A holiday and weekend home from home that will fit easily into quite a small vehicle and won't need something the size of an aircraft hangar for storage. Youngsters too may like their own small inexpensive ridge or dome.

In the days when the size of house and car grew with

Smaller for transportation -
Marechal Vis-à-Vis 4 berth

the number of children the family tent followed the same pattern. These days few people change car and tent each year. Many of us are making do with a more compact house or flat and a smaller and more economical car and the tent cloth has to be cut accordingly. This is one area where lightweight tents come into their own. They are not only smaller for transportation but relatively inexpensive to buy. These cheaper tents may not last a family for several generations like a cotton frame model and without adequate ventilation there may be a certain amount of condensation, but the key word here is compromise and we must weigh up the pros and cons. As with all tents the fabric, guylines, stitching and pegging point rubber bands should be inspected from time to time and certainly before the annual holiday.

If the family expands you might need two smaller tents. There are few 6 berth models that are high, wide and lightweight although the Lichfield Challenger Royale made in cotton or nylon is designed to sleep 5. (Don't forget if you use two tents the campsite may ask for two separate pitch fees.)

Retired people who have given up caravanning are also taking to camping again for a variety of reasons, such as difficulty in dealing with towing and lack of space to keep a caravan. The tent has become an attractive substitute, especially when that's how their love of the outdoor life grew in the first place.

Lightweight tents too are great for a touring holiday - and as mentioned you're not restricted to one tent. Depending on the size of the car it's possible to 'double up' and save on petrol - take one car across the channel instead of two saving quite a large amount.

For instance three adults in our family went off to Northern Italy recently. We took one Ford Fiesta J reg car, one Lichfield Challenger Classic XL5 nylon tent and one Marechal Turbo 3 in proofed polyester. The reason I mention the year of the car is that the boot is more generous than in the earlier models.

We also took a table and chairs, air beds, sleeping bags, double burner, cool bag and a hibachi barbecue. The spare back seat was used for sleeping bags and rucksack containing clothes. No trailer, no roof rack and we could still use the rear view mirror. This 'stow it all in' type of camping needs some organizing and neat packing but because none of the equipment was particularly heavy it was quite feasible and cost saving.

The tents we took, when pitched, were on the large size with plenty of headroom. Comfortable camping was our aim, it was not our intention to

In proofed polyester

'rough it'. If you want to cut down on the size of the tent bags there are other lightweight dome tents which we'll come to later. Look for one with a porch and windows or the comfort we're concentrating on will be lost.

LIGHTWEIGHT TOURER, DOME OR RIDGE?

Much of the advice on materials, inner tent and living space mentioned in the previous chapter on frame tents applies to lightweight models - although there won't be a kitchen annexe and dimensions in the main are scaled down.

Most lightweight tents are made from nylon with a few in polyester. We can't tell the difference. They are both proofed, both need good ventilation, they both fold up into a small package and will dry off quickly.

So what is the difference between an extended dome and an extended ridge and what should we look for? Well of course, to begin with, shape and method of pitching. It's difficult to generalize but living space in a chalet is likely to be more generous while head and elbow room in the inner of a dome may be better. This comparison is immediately thrown on to the campfire if we put a Marechal Super Nomade multi dome against their AP3 Canadienne with windows. Living space in the first is 285 x 215cm, in

Lightweight vis-à vis in dome style

the second only 170 x 90cm.

If the brochure gives a maximum height take a look at the doorway. If it is lower than the central dome some back bending may be necessary as you step inside.

Basically there are two types of quick and easy to erect lightweight tents that may be suitable for small family camping. (There are a few exceptions which we'll come to later.) One, the high dome, uses a series of shock cord linked glass fibre poles or rods in two (or more) easy to assemble main sections. These are simply crossed over with the ends being fitted into eyelets attached to the inner's groundsheet. The other, pitched in ridge style, is often called a chalet tent. Both will probably be extended by extra polework to make a porch or living area and windows will be provided.

In the case of the dome there may be a third arched section over the porch to give extra height and/or a canopy which is made up from the door flap. This can sometimes be held out by aluminium poles and guylines. An example here is the Marechal Turbo 3 and 4.

Going larger again there are some designs which use two or more domes, perhaps in the vis-à-vis style. The latter has one sleeping compartment at each side of a living area giving a little more privacy - for instance the Lichfield Condor.

Watch height and width, remember that the larger the tent the more wind resistance - these high and wide tents are not meant for exposed sites or mountain tops, although we're not saying they couldn't cope. All tents depend on good pitching, pegging and secure guylines for their stability.

Much will depend on the weather. In a hot dry country where you don't expect rain, meals can be taken al fresco anyway. But as many of us have found out you can't always rely on the past records of certain countries and for comfort your quick and easy to erect tourer should have an enclosed porch or living area of some kind.

Framework for chalet style tents is based on a central ridge pole which is extended right out to the front wall. Other poles are then attached to make a T shape with the front porch being held out by the top of the T. In other words as few poles as possible with shape and stability depending on the pegging out of the flysheet or outer tent.

This might be a good point to explain that domes can be pitched by one person but extended ridges really need two people. Not because the tent is heavy or particularly awkward but the ridge pole might be at least 12ft long, going from the back wall to the front door. There are usually two side uprights to give height at the door and in the living area and the whole framework needs steadying while the flysheet is thrown over. Just a hand or two should do, little strength is required.

INNER TENTS

The inner compartment of a dome is similar in style to that in a frame tent. A chalet or extended ridge will have a ridge style inner but with more headroom than usual. In both there will be a sewn-in groundsheet, a zipped door and in most a mesh ventilator. If you need to keep out midges make sure the model you choose uses a really closely woven ventilator material. Some will only keep out flies and mosquitoes. The type of doorway too would have to be considered.

For full protection from mosquitoes etc. you'll need one of the specialist tents where the manufacturer has thoroughly researched the subject from jungle to mountain top, but these do not normally come under the Family Camping heading.

When sizing up the inner, bear in mind the roof shape of the dome and the ridge. We're thinking here about sitting up in bed to drink the early morning cuppa and getting dressed. This is what I call 'elbow room' and all adds to or detracts from camping comfort.

For two or three people this aspect was excellent in the Lichfield Challenger Classic XL5, although if the suggested four people were using the inner compartment there might have been a few elbows nudged and several spilt drinks. Although it's highly unlikely that mum, dad and two children will sit in a line like birds on a fence, sipping their morning drinks. It will probably be a case of on with the shorts and top and over to the cornflake packet or out to the swings and slide!

We aim to give the would-be camper an idea of the game or pastime and some food for thought. The advice in Chapter One still applies. Try to choose a larger tent than the manufacturer says it is designed for. As long as the dome or ridge inner is of good height in the first place and you don't try to squash in too many bodies the sloping walls shouldn't be much of a problem.

LIVING AREA OR PORCH

For comfort the larger the better in height, width and depth. If you only need room for boots and a couple of rucksacks a small area may be sufficient. It's unlikely that a table and chairs will fit into a single dome tent although two small seats might be all right, perhaps using a small coffee table. It's true to say that you may feel more relaxed sitting on the ground anyway. It's surprising how quickly this basic sitting position becomes quite natural - although that's what many of us are trying to avoid. On the other hand I'm sure there are families who revel in the type of camping they learnt in the Scouts and Guides.

There's something very cosy about a tent without windows but if like me you want to see what you're eating as well as what your neighbours look like then windows are part of the tent's comfort. Extended domes will usually have two or more as will extended ridges. Curtains do not usually come as part of the package and may not even be offered. The Lichfield Challenger Classic XL5 is one exception, where curtains are an optional extra.

Marechal makes several really large domes such as the Super Nomade 3 and 4. These are provided with two doorways. One is a roll up panel in a side wall. The other door flap can be stretched out and held in place by aluminium poles and guylines to be used as a canopy. If you wanted to use a table and chairs it's possible to keep the main door closed. Again it would depend on the number of occupants and the weather.

POLEWORK MATERIALS

Dome poles might be made of glass fibre or alloy. On some Lichfield models the glass fibre rods come as standard and alloy poles are an optional extra. Whether they are worth the extra £15 or so we can't say. With my family team I evaluate many tents for camping magazines and The Camping and Caravanning Club but we don't get the chance to use the tents for long enough to find out the lasting qualities of the poles or canvas. With tents that we actually own we have never experienced any problems with glass fibre poles but some campers wouldn't use anything other than alloy dome rods.

One important point here is that if you buy a tent and use it as per instructions and it fails in some way - take it back to the retailer. Manufacturers can't get away with shoddy goods these days.

Most of the glass fibre and alloy poles are hollow with shock cording to connect them, in other words with a kind of elastic linking. Solid glass fibre poles seem to have been gradually phased out. They are a bit of a fiddle to manoeuvre. As the bone-like rods were being threaded through their channel in the flysheet they could too easily come apart and after a long day's drive and/or if it's raining you want the tent ready for use in as short a time as possible.

The way lightweight tent inners are attached to the flysheet is interesting. In some models, and these are usually the smaller tents, the glass fibre or alloy poles are threaded through a sleeve or channel in the flysheet material. The ferruled ends then fit into metal or nylon eyelets attached to tongues at each side. This way the outer can be pitched first and the inner is then pegged and a series of hooks on the roof of the inner are attached to O rings on the inside of the flysheet.

Another method is to pitch inner first and this seems to be the most popular with manufacturers and we're inclined to go along with that. Not so good if it's raining but when clips on the outside of the inner's roof are used the tent can be erected very quickly. When comparing these two methods it's sometimes a matter of whether the erector or the inner tent gets wet if the weather is bad.

It must quickly be said, however, that with practice these small tents can be pitched in double quick time, whichever method is used. Remember to examine the complete package, whether you decide on a large or small tent. If there are lots of bits and pieces erecting may take longer. On the other hand it may be just these extras that make for that little extra comfort. And there our case rests.

Camping at Arolla in
the Swiss Alps - close
to nature in wonderful
surroundings.
 Photo: R.B.Evans

Relum Izmir Pyramid (Chapter 1)

Above: France is an ideal venue for a family car-camping holiday . Numerous well run sites close to attractive old towns and villages make touring a real pleasure. This is at Crest in the Drôme, note the castle in the background. *Photo: R.B. Evans*

Lichfield Montana 4 with optional canopy (Chapter 1)

ALTERNATIVE TOURERS

Exceptions to the basic dome or ridge shape are to be found in several catalogues and from time to time a company will bring out a single design that it hopes will revolutionise the 'quick and easy' tent market. The Igloo, with inflatable roof 'poles', was one. Many of these were sold but it's some years since they were available. Others come and go like birds to a feeding table, some of them never to appear again.

The Raclet Quicktent, a cotton tent with the frame on the outside, has been around for some years. In the style of a pram hood and some trailer tents, the frame is simply pulled 'up and over' - that is, after it has been laid in position and corner pegged. Then final pegging takes place. The inner is already in position and the Quicktent is taken down in reverse order. The canvas and inner are folded up like a parcel and back it goes into its kitbag.

Measuring 7ft 10in in width this would be a 2 or 3 berth. Manufacturers seem to vary between 18in and 24in when estimating the sleeping space for each person. If using air beds measure up first. Lichfield suggests that four people can fit into the 8ft (224cm) of their Challenger 5 and Challenger XL5. The Raclet Quicktent could certainly be described as a touring tent, but at 18kg it is relatively heavy and at 46 x 10in diameter the package is not exactly compact. However this touring tent has good headroom at 6ft 2in and is a useful addition to the camping scene.

Another tent or portable shelter when talking 'light' is the Caranex. A kind of car annexe, there are several sizes with models to fit most hatchbacks including the Toyota Landcruiser and other 'off roaders'. With floor space of 7ft 6in x 5ft on all models the Caranex really only sleeps two. However, as with others in this 'alternative' section it is well worth a mention. Weighing just 11lbs, at 6ft 4in it is full height and can be quickly assembled.

Erecting is very simple. Two wooden spacers are used for the roof and there are two aluminium legs. The tent is simply laid out behind the vehicle, the Caranex body is brought 'up and over' and the legs positioned. There's no inner tent to worry about but a privacy curtain is provided for the space between hatchback and tent. The hatchback can be opened and used. One drawback of an annexe is that if you want to drive out for the evening the tent has to be detached although a free standing kit is available for the Caranex.

The series of tents that may have revolutionised camping is the Khyam One Touch Range. Their claim is 'erected start to finish in 20 seconds'. The frame is of solid glass fibre poles with hinged plastic joints which just leap together.

There are several 4 person models in igloo and tunnel shapes. The latest, the Mega Dome, could be the one to interest the family camper. Said to sleep 4-6 it measures 345cm at the widest point, weighs 8.2kg, has a packed size of 110 x 24cm and a grand height of over 6ft.

Most manufacturers' catalogues show a range of smaller dome tents, with and without windows. Those that interest the family camper are the straightforward single domes that let in plenty of light. Names of these 3-4 berth that spring to mind are the Freeman Apollo, Lichfield Osprey and Regatta Sherpa. They do not have full height doors but headroom is quite good. Pitching is quick and easy because there are only two main cross-over sections. Windows are provided and the porch is held out either by a third glass fibre arch or two aluminium uprights.

Single domes are worth looking at for touring and youngsters may like the idea of taking their own small tent. When it comes to the basic dome without a porch the choice is wide and many of these come into the 'specialist' category. Some can be very expensive. Models for the non-mountaineer can be bought at a more reasonable price. There may be a small canopy which will help to keep the rain off the zip and doorway. And lastly, the ever popular ridge, a quick and simple to pitch tent that many people, and especially youngsters, still see as the only 'real' tent.

'The ridge is not for family camping' you may be saying, but don't dismiss the large ridge style altogether. It may well have the space and height you need and a lack of frills and flounces and separate inners means that pitching will not take hours. Relum make the Pearl and Giant Pearl with a height of 6ft suitable for 4 and 6 people. Both are in tough, hard wearing cotton, have sewn-in groundsheets and weigh 27lb (12kg)and 33lb (15kg) respectively.

CHAPTER THREE

Erecting a tent

FRAME

Three important points come to mind when talking about erecting a frame tent. Safety, a trial run, and a reminder not to forget the mallet. By safety we mean distance between tents and leaving sufficient space in case of fire. (Picking the right pitch will be covered in Chapter Six.) On a site with marked out pitches, especially those with shrubs or a hedge on three sides, much of the guesswork will be taken away. Even then the tent needs to be

Get to know the polework

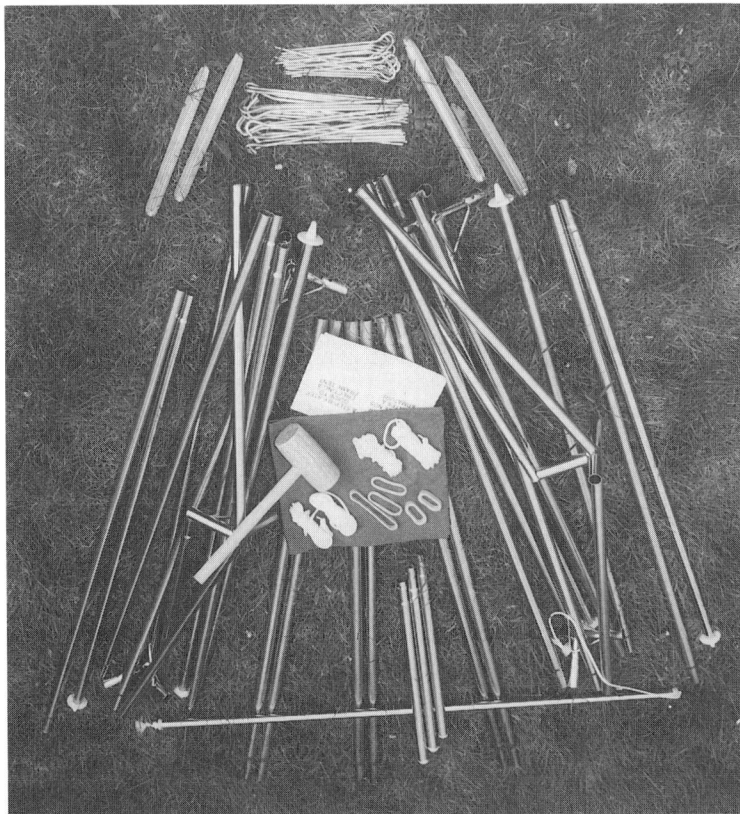

pitched centrally or you could find your guylines tangled up with those of your neighbours if the foliage is sparse. Remember to distance the rear wall of the tent if the pitches are back to back.

Marked pitches vary a lot in size but as a guide to safe pitching the Camping and Outdoor Leisure Association in their *Equipment and Clothing Care* leaflet (which is issued with many new tents) suggest 'a minimum of 6m between adjacent tents or awnings'. The Camping and Caravanning Club in their *Club Handbook* state 'units, excluding guy ropes, must be 20 feet apart from adjacent units'.

That trial run. Start at the very beginning and READ THE INSTRUCTIONS in the comfort of your own armchair. Most manufacturers' guarantees will be invalid if these are not meticulously followed. There's nothing difficult about erecting a frame tent but you do need to get to know the polework. Some retailers will go through this with you but in the excitement of buying a new tent it's not always easy to remember what went where.

Not many of us like to give a theatre performance when we arrive on site. If your garden is large enough then erect the tent there. If there's no room for the full canvas and guyropes there may be space to try out the frame. Then pick a quiet campsite and go away for a weekend. Arrival on a campsite in France after a hard day's drive is not the time to find there is a pole missing. It can happen.

The instructions may or may not make absolute sense to begin with, especially if they are written in a language unknown to us, which could even be Polish. However, common sense, the line drawings and photographs usually provided - along with this book - will give you a good idea of the whole procedure. Things will become even clearer when you check the frame and all the bits and pieces such as guylines, pegs and any extra poles needed for kitchen annexe, hanging wardrobe, curtains etc. The Midlands-based Lichfield company come out tops in this respect. They include a list of contents in their tent packages which means you don't even need to know the shape of the frame before ticking off the poles.

Mentioning the mallet may sound unneccessary at this point but think of the toy without a battery and the kitchen flatpack without a screwdriver. It's true, campers are a friendly bunch and there would be a mallet somewhere on site. We forgot to take saucepans and a kettle on our first ever camping trip but we didn't go hungry or without a cuppa! In fact borrowing the proverbial 'cup of sugar' might be a good way of getting to know other campers. I'll leave it to the reader.

Whether or not a tent manufacturer should include a mallet with a new tent has been a subject for discussion ever since the frame tent was introduced. Very few manufacturers include one these days, Cabanon and Lichfield probably being the exceptions. Those supplied will be wooden mallets and capable of doing the job.

It has to be said though that we prefer a rubber headed mallet with a steel shaft. This means that even if one is provided with the tent we don't use it! Is this where the manufacturer's case rests? The rubber head has a certain amount of spring causing less jarring of the elbow if the ground is hard.

Some campers say they never use a mallet. 'What's wrong with the foot for pressing in a peg?' First of all if the ground is rock-like, which can happen in hot weather, on well used pitches with packed down earth, almost anywhere, the peg needs more than a shoe.

Safety too is important here. I've seen a peg being pushed down 'by foot' go straight through the sole of a shoe - ouch! Pushing in with the foot can also ruin the pegs. They might go in all right, bending over as they are levered down, but once bent they become very difficult to drive home and remove unless the ground is soft.

So you've checked the contents, read the instructions and are raring to go. You unpack the bags. There's usually one containing the outer canvas, one the poles and sometimes a third, and then the Chinese puzzle that sits at your feet may cause panic. Don't worry. Some of the larger jumbles fit

A simple frame at half or kneeling height - Cabanon Elzas IV

Push button adjusters

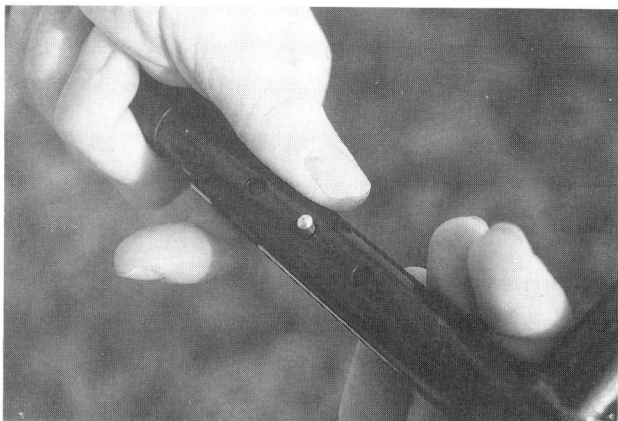

together as easily as a wooden jigsaw puzzle. The French company Cabanon is good at this. Its frames seem to be connected to make as few main sections as possible. They almost spring together on their own and if you remember that the three short canopy stubs must face front, erecting should be a quick and simple affair.

Frame tent polework, whether steel or alloy, all looks much the same and assembling the poles does not vary a lot but there are differences. Most poles will have spring linking which makes identification easier and keeps the poles together. Some are only partly linked.

Some manufacturers provide press button adjusters where the legs meet up with the roof corner brackets. These might have two or three different positions. The instructions usually state which set should be used when first assembling the frame - the canvas might shrink slightly. Press button adjusters are also an aid to getting the canvas to sit squarely on uneven ground.

If the upright/corner joints are loose, with no linking, the legs may drop out at the wrong moment. These are usually supplied with budget priced tents and if you've saved quite a few pounds they may be worth the slight inconvenience. Erecting a frame tent soon becomes as easy as brewing a cup of tea and I know at least one salesman who can, on his own, pitch a 6 berth and be ready to drink a cup in about as much time as it takes to boil the kettle.

First of all clear the pitch of any sharp stones or twigs as you don't want the groundsheet and air beds punctured. It's a good idea to protect the groundsheet of the inner with a square of polythene or a separate groundsheet bought for a few pounds at a camping shop or centre. Don't use ordinary polythene in the living area as it can be slippery. Then lay out the frame roughly in the position you think it should go.

The roof sections and corner brackets will show themselves, as will the cross pieces for the roof. Position these with short canopy sections, usually three in number, where you want the front doorway to be. The legs or uprights are easy to identify because these usually have a nylon or plastic foot. Extra poles may be for the kitchen annexe and the long slim pole with an attached cord is the wardrobe rail. Once the frame is laid out in front of you the connecting can begin.

The legs will be in several linked sections and once the whole frame has been assembled it should be left at a 'half height' or 'kneeling' position. That is, with the lower ends of the legs disconnected and splayed out. If you had been wondering how you were going to position the canvas when the tent is 7ft high your puzzle is now solved.

At this kneeling height it should be easy enough to lay the outer canvas over the roof frame. Make sure the outside is on the right side and that the canopy stubs are threaded through their bound apertures in the front wall. Lift up the 12in or more of the front canopy to find them.

At this point, before raising the frame to its full height, and depending on your own stature, it may be necessary to suspend the inner tent or tents. This is another aspect that will be worked out as you get to know your frame tent. Keep the canvas off the ground if you can as it's bound to get grubby in the long run, although it's surprising how clean canvas can be kept.

If the tent is provided with corner tapes on the inside of the canvas this is the time - especially if its windy - to tie them to the frame but in bows and loosely at first. If they're too tight at this stage the tent may not sit on the frame properly. If you decide to tighten there and then make sure the corner of the canvas is sitting squarely on the frame bracket. Don't tug at the tapes but move the canvas.

Next raise the frame to full height. The canvas is best left folded until the last minute but if it does fall down make sure none of the material gets trapped under the uprights - and don't trip over the splayed out legs as you check!

Although one person can erect a basic 2 berth frame tent and even larger this does put strain on the polework which could be a bad thing, especially if it's made of alloy. It doesn't seem to matter whether the two side or two front legs are raised first but if there are two erectors make sure your lifting movements are synchronized. If it's really blowing a gale you can attach the guylines at the kneeling stage leaving enough cord for the tent to be lifted to its final position. Again, practice makes perfect.

If the tent walls have not fallen down into place go round and arrange the canvas in its final position. Make sure the outer is sitting squarely. The legs may need moving in or out slightly - gently does it.

Before starting the final pegging out, all door and window zips should be closed. Once pegged never force a door zip. If the tent does shrink in the early days move a few pegs so that the zip moves freely. Some manufacturers recommend final pegging before suspending the inners, others afterwards. Either way the tent can be generally tidied up when all parts are in position. If the pitch slopes or is uneven you may not get the tent to look like the picture in the brochure but moving pegs will help. The lower edge of the tent should be pegged out taught enough for rain to run off but not so tight that the rubber rings are stretched out. The look will tell you if its right.

How well the tent is going to keep out the rain and how well it will cope in a gale will depend on the taughtness of the canvas as well as the pegging out and the correct positioning of the guylines. If pegging points along the walls are left out there could be a draught or worse. Not only will the noise of flapping canvas be annoying, in a gale it could be a matter of 'one out, all out' as once the wind takes hold a row of pegs could be ripped out.

If the roof is allowed to sag inwards a puddle can form and eventually the water will drip through. No matter what the weather is like at the time of erecting the tent it's a good idea to use all pegging points and every single guyline. That sun and blue sky can become cloud and breeze in a short time. Check on the quality of the guylines - they may need to be changed for a tougher variety.

Don't let these warnings worry you too much. It never ceases to surprise us the amount of bad weather several yards of canvas or nylon and a few poles and pegs can withstand. New canvas does need to be 'weathered' though. The fibres of cotton canvas are not exactly sealed. A shower of rain is all you need, which will expand the threads leaving no space for water to get through. During the first rainfall there may only be a fine spray or you may not notice it at all. Several heavy morning dews may serve the same purpose as a downpour. If you decide that 'weathering' should take place before that first camping trip the tent should be fully pitched and pegged to stop the canvas from changing shape as it dries. Take it easy, a hose and hot sun are not recommended. Tents have been known to shrink as much as 6in. Imagine a sweatshirt if you hung it out to dry with one sleeve stretched out. It would stay several inches longer until washed again.

It's worth pointing out that proofed nylon does not shrink until it has first stretched. In other words when nylon gets wet it stretches - and looks quite bedraggled. Any spray on the inside will be condensation from the body or cooking. Nylon fabric dries quite quickly and then shrinks back to its original size.

Take things easy when you first erect a frame tent. New campers who try to rush the procedure can be quite a problem for retailers. Poles get bent, in severe cases canvas can be torn. Don't use brute force. If a pole is being awkward stand back and think 'is it in the right place?' As regular testers of frame and other types of tent our team always makes a cup of tea and takes a break if things aren't going too well. Yes it can happen to us. Some tents are prototypes with no instructions, others are new to the country and the translation is still at the printer! French and German we can deal with but Polish or Dutch are a different matter. After a short rest and a pooling of thoughts the tent usually goes up as quickly as an umbrella.

A supply of pegs will be provided with the frame tent. This will usually consist of a number of 9in steel pegs (perhaps four even larger for the corners) for the outer canvas and some 6in for the inner. If angle pegs are supplied, these will probably number 4 and will be for the corners of the outer.

One company stands out when it comes to tent pegs: Relum of Czechoslovakia. It provides a range of tough, heavy pegs that would challenge any wind and sandy pitch. Relum is also one of the few companies to provide squares of material for repairs. In 25 years we've never needed a patch but these could be useful if an area of mould eats into the fabric or you are unfortunate enough to sustain a tear.

Most manufacturers provide sufficient pegs for the tent - just. Take some spares though. They do get lost and stony ground can bend them into corkscrews even when a mallet is used. If those supplied do not appear to be strong enough, look at some alternatives. Ask the advice of your retailer as he may have a range of nylon or plastic pegs and will know which are duds. Some can be brittle and shatter, others are looked upon by some campers as being the best thing since sewn-in groundsheets. We use a mixture.

Peg out in the order recommended in the instructions. Cross-pegging is advisable at zipped doorways. This means putting in the pegs but crossing over the rubber rings. This will keep the lower ends of the zip together. Relum also use a large hook and eye at this point which has a similar effect.

The actual angle of the hammered in peg should also be considered if it is going to stay in position. The normal advice is a 90 degree angle against

Peg should be positioned at a 90 degree angle against the direction of pull

the direction of pull. If the peg sits upright it will pull out easily. Too shallow and it will lift up taking a patch of grass with it.

If you buy a Cabanon tent the plastic or nylon D ring next to the pegging rubber may confuse you. This is a kind of emergency point for attaching replacement rubber rings.

It's some years since we've seen another row of pegging holes on the outer edge of a mudflap. If you do come across them they are probably best left alone or only pegged lightly with the mudflap not being stretched in any way.

Suspending the inner tent or tents is a simple procedure. The type of roof clips and pegging points may vary slightly. To get a good fit we've tried attaching roof clips first and we've tried pegging out first. As with the outer, much will depend on the undulation or otherwise of the pitch. Make sure there's a space between outer and inner wall, if they're touching the roof or walls may leak. Juggle the pegs and clips around and find out which position makes the inner compartment look 'comfortable'. Too much tension may cause tearing of walls, ventilators or pegging points. If you find that the rubber rings that attach clips to roof poles are on the tight side add another one - and carry spares anyway.

With luxury frame tents you may not have finished erecting yet. Curtains grace the front and possibly side windows of most frame tents. Warm looking roof liners, with pelmets which cover up the space between the top of the inner and the roof of the outer are available in an increasing number of models. There may even be a curtain around the kitchen annexe although I feel these could be a fire hazard. Add the bits and pieces, walk round and if necessary adjust any pegs, and your detached property is ready for occupation.

Inner of 'extended ridge' or 'chalet'

Pitching a twin-ridge

CHALET OR EXTENDED RIDGE

The same initial stages of pitching a frame tent also apply to the chalet or extended ridge (see opposite p32 top). Clear the pitch and use a separate groundsheet if possible. Some nylon tents have an extra lightweight groundsheet. This may be to save on the ounces or it may be to save cash, whichever, it always seems so vulnerable. We're not writing for backpackers who need all their gear to be as light as possible and would advise an extra layer between the ground and your air beds, either a groundsheet or heavy duty polythene.

The ridge style inner compartment of a chalet is usually pitched first. The inner is simply laid out and the corners pegged. Two uprights are then positioned inside the inner, one back and one front. Spikes at the top of these 'legs' then go through eyelets in the roof to meet up with a ridge pole. Remember to read the instructions. There will probably be a couple of 4 or 5in lengths of hollow metal spacers. These go over the spike between outer and flysheet to stop the two materials touching. There may also be a loop on the outside of the inner's roof so don't forget to thread the ridge pole through before attaching the ends to the uprights.

Polework for the living area varies. In a straightforward chalet the flysheet is positioned and there will be two uprights with spikes which go through holes over the doorway. The windows are at the side of this and these front 'legs' are held in place by guylines. The door in this case is unzipped at each side and rolled up.

Lichfield, as far as we know, is the only company to have taken the full height chalet design a few stages further with its Challenger Royale and Challenger Classic. A curved zip door makes these designs more frame-like, providing more full height comfort. It's possible to unzip and walk into the 'lounge' instead of having to roll up a door flap. The Classic and the Royale require two more uprights and two roof struts to make up the front walls but the great thing here is that these tents are in lightweight nylon and still relatively quick and easy to erect. Finally the flysheet of all the chalet style tents is pegged out and guylines attached.

DOMES

Dome tents are so quick and easy to pitch that the notes in Chapter Two - (Lightweights) have probably covered the whole procedure. As with the chalet style the inner is first pegged out. Reinforced pvc tongues with nylon eyelets are provided at each corner of the inner, which take the ends

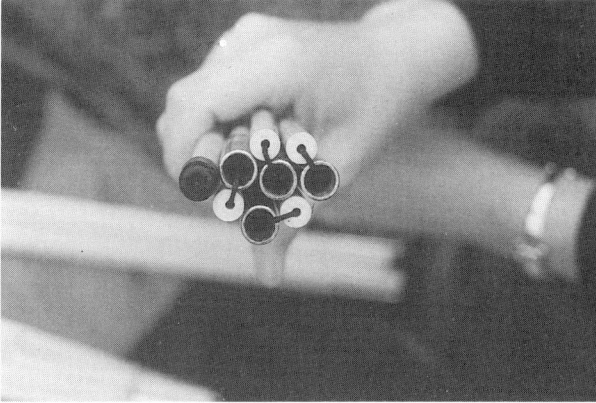

Glass fibre dome rods
with shockcord
linking

of the two glass fibre dome sections. As the dome is made up from a series
of rods all linked by elasticated cord there are no worries about what goes
where.

The inner is then lifted and the roof clips are attached to the dome poles.
Don't take this as universal though, as sometimes there are loops on the
inner roof which means the poles have to be threaded through before being
fitted into their corner tongues. There may be strips of Velcro fastening on
the inside of the flysheet which simply go round the poles.

There may be a third arched section or two uprights to be held out by
guylines, either of which will make a porch. Super domes such as those
made by Marechal may have a fourth hooped pole to make quite an
elongated extension.

Erecting a vis-à-vis dome tent is 'as before' except that there will be two
inners. All the dome styles follow the same pattern. Establish exactly
which holes in the corner tongues are meant to take a rod and which is for
a peg. This should just be a case of trial and error - or reading the
instructions.

DISMANTLING

Dismantling takes place in the reverse order. Dry off the tent as much as
possible and clean the groundsheet. (Dry off thoroughly for storage.) Lay
out the bag and size up the folds to fit. The folded package is then rolled
up, pressing out any trapped air as you go, and slipped into the kitbag.
Some manufacturers provide a generous size valise, others don't seem to
worry what happens on the return journey. This usually goes with the
price paid. Folding the tent correctly will come with practice.

CHAPTER FOUR

Camping Equipment

The list of available camping equipment is as long as several guylines. Luxury additions such as a toaster that can be used on a gas burner can be left for a later date. However some campers need to experience the whole scene with maximum comfort on that first trip. If anyone in the party is not at all sure about setting up home at the side of a field all possible luxuries should be there from day one.

A comfortable bed and bedding are perhaps the most important pieces of camping gear, followed by a kitchen unit with a two burner stove and table and chairs. In the early days you can take cutlery, crockery and pots and pans from your kitchen and in good weather the duvets from home may be suitable.

The latter is not always a good idea as new air beds can leave a distinct smell of rubber clinging to them. The evocative smells of camping such as crushed grass, canvas proofer and frying bacon can be hard to beat but we don't necessarily want to be tucked up in bed with them when the holiday break is over. Covers are easy enough to wash but do you want to deal with the quilts after each weekend? Sleeping bags are warmer and more comfortable all round. If camping is going to become a regular family activity - and it can become addictive - the answer is a separate set of gear stored in one place so that the vehicle can be easily packed at short notice.

AIR AND CAMP BEDS, SLEEPING MATS AND COTS

Most campers find inflatable air beds more comfortable than fold away camp beds. There's no cold air space between groundsheet and body, they are more stable and it's possible to snuggle down for some of the most restful nights of your life.

Air beds are available in the reeded type - lilo style - and box-sided like your bed at home. Choose the waffle pattern for maximum comfort as it's easier to roll off the reeded ones. Both are made with and without an inflatable pillow. With an attached pillow all you need to take is a pillow case. This has to open at one side instead of at the end though. Ours were made from an old sheet.

My own preference is a box-sided air bed with a proper pillow. Decisions,

decisions, do you have space in the camping vehicle? Another option is to take separate blow-up pillows. Scatter cushions could be useful as long as they're not 'springy' enough to take off during the night.

ALTERNATIVE BEDS - AND COTS

Some campers insist on sleeping 'off the floor'. With today's sewn-in groundsheets and zipped up inner compartments this is not as crucial as it used to be. If inner doors are kept closed at night it's highly unlikely that creepy crawlies will be a problem - but fold-up camp beds are still available. Sun loungers are not really suitable as they can tip up unless the sleeper turns over very carefully.

Sleeping mats as used by backpackers which can either be self-inflating or just a layer of special foam are light and can be rolled into a small package. Perhaps not as cosy as a conventional air bed but I find the self-inflating kind fine for short trips and there's no pumping up at the end of a day's drive. True, I sometimes roll off that and wonder why I bother because I've slept through the night even though cuddled up on the unfriendly groundsheet! If you are going for lightweight camping, say in a small car or motor cycle and using one of the nylon tents, camping mats may be the answer.

If you've already bought the tent, measure up the inner before picking out the beds. Just because the tent is called a 4 berth doesn't mean it will necessarily take four air or camp beds.

Only the reader can decide at what age children should be taken camping (more in Chapter Five). A folding travel cot with high see-through mesh sides may be already part of your life. The Mothercare chain

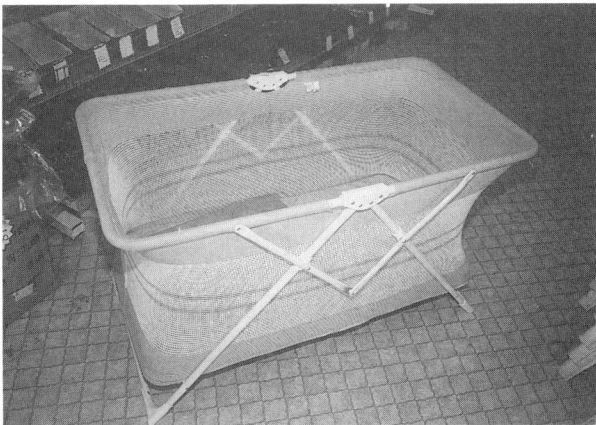

Travel cot with mesh sides

47

stock them - you can buy by mail order - and camping shops usually have a choice available.

FOOT PUMPS, DOME PUMPS, ELECTRIC PUMPS

When it comes to pumping up the air beds there are several alternatives, the most popular over the years being the simple dome type made from rubber. There's a Swedish version that should involve half the effort because it inflates on both the up and the down stroke and Coleman make an electric pump that is operated from the car's cigar lighter.

You may already have a boat inflator in which case make sure you also take a nozzle of the right size. My car foot pump was supplied with a separate plastic attachment which I realised some years later would do the job. It is not advisable to blow up air beds by mouth. Apart from being unhygienic the moisture from the breath doesn't do the bed any good either.

SLEEPING BAGS

Choosing a sleeping bag is rather like picking out a second-hand car. You may read all the paperwork imaginable, ask around, decide on the best model and then find it isn't available in your area. In this case, be guided by your local outdoor shop or centre. As with any other gear, today's consumer laws put pressure on the retailers to stock decent marketable products. In other words if the retailers have had complaints or returned products they won't stock them again. No-one enjoys the angry customer. This doesn't mean the most expensive has to be the most suitable for the job. We do get what we pay for but savings can be made and it's a good idea to do some research first.

There's no such thing as the 'best sleeping bag'. Why spend out for an expensive high spec model that can be used on an Arctic expedition if you're going to the south of France in August? It might not be a lot of good anyway although a cotton liner on its own may be - if one is taken (more on liners later).

Certain questions have to be asked. Where will the bag be used? Mountain top, sun-kissed beach and so on? When will it be expected to function - all year round, from Easter to October or just in summer months? With an increasing number of campsites opening well into the autumn a 3 season bag might be the best idea. Country days in September, October, April and May can be superb so don't pack the camping gear away too early. Just consider the cooler nights when looking at sleeping bags. In

Above: Lichfield Challenger 5. Reasonably priced nylon lightweight for a small family
Below: Ariel Twin Ridge (Chapter 2)

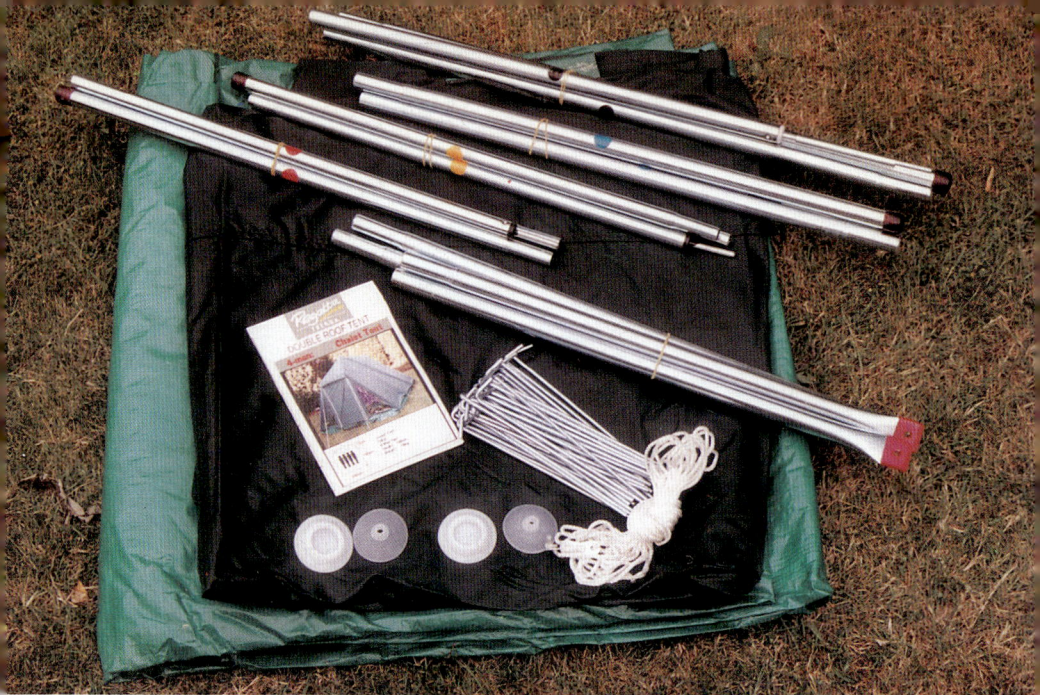

Above:
Chalet style lightweight
- the complete package,
flysheet and polework.
(Chapter 3)

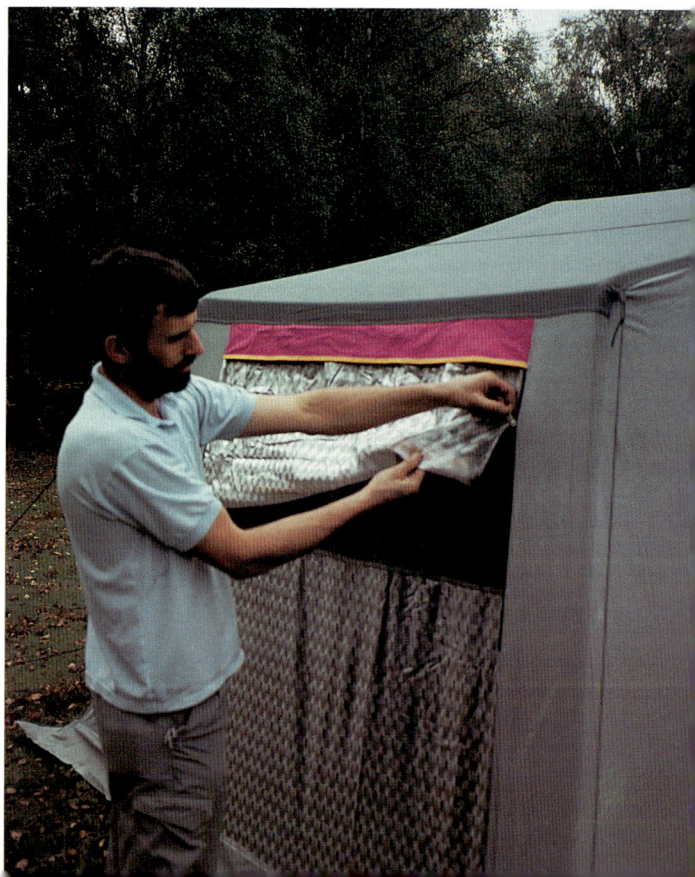

Right:
Push-out kitchen panel
(Chapter 1)

some cases a temperature rating of say -12°C is given, in others 2/3-season and so on.

Most family campers will choose a bag made with a synthetic fibre filling. The cover may be of cotton, polycotton or nylon, the lining usually cotton or polycotton. The advantages of synthetics are that they dry quicker and the fillings retain much of their insulating capacity even if damp. They also cost less than down. The design too makes a difference as to how well the filling will function. If it's allowed to slip about or bunch up there will be cold spots.

If you ask the advice of a backpacker he may say 'go for a down bag'. The main reason is that down will pack into a small parcel and weigh very little. If space is limited, down could be the only answer. Down and feathers do have disadvantages though. They are more sensitive to moisture and can go lumpy in which case some of the insulating properties would then be lost. In the main down is more expensive than synthetics.

Night-time just about anywhere can be cold at times. Jogging suit pyjamas can be very handy if you intend to camp at either ends of the

Sleeping bags - get the right style and filling for the job

season - or at any other time of the year if the weather is chilly. Very few of us can afford to buy both summer and winter sleeping bags so medium weight models combined with warm sleeping wear is a good compromise. Taking a spare blanket or two is another option.

At first glance you may think it's going to be a lonely night in a sleeping bag with your partner also zipped up like a mummy. Never fear, look for 'convertibles' which can be used as singles or zipped together as a double.

Special children's size sleeping bags with cute covers may be attractive but will be outgrown very quickly. We don't want the youngsters sliding down into the bag's depths though. I've heard of campers using a strap or length of rope tied tightly round the bottom section of an adult bag until the child has grown into it but have had no personal experience.

We won't go into all the different makes and types of sleeping bag fillings. The Camping and Outdoor Centre (formerly Scout Shops) with 21 branches around the country (plus a mail order operation) issue a very informative leaflet with an 'at a glance' Season Usage Chart. The YHA publish a similar guide (see appendix for addresses).

Sleeping bag liners can be bought or made from old sheets but even though they are much easier to wash than the complete bag we haven't yet found anyone who regularly uses them. How many times will the user turn in the night? I began to feel like a bandaged up corkscrew. If you're used to a sheet sleeping bag at a Youth Hostel there may be no problem.

TABLE AND CHAIRS

A table and chairs are essential if we're going for 'maximum comfort' camping. Family eating habits have changed a lot. Two adult and two

Chairs are essential for comfort

children's size chairs used to be the 'norm' for a family of four. Many of us have become adept at eating meals from our laps but this could be messy for small children and who wants to be washing clothes after every meal?

Strangely, eating out of doors has moved in the opposite direction to TV meals and has become a much more civilised affair. Well, a table set with a bottle of wine and stylish melamine crockery looks a touch more elegant than plastic plates and a chianti bottle rolling around the grass! 'Roughing it' does not come into the modern camping vocabulary.

The questions to be asked are: How many people will be sitting down at the table? Will several of them be children? How big is the living area, will there be enough space in tent and in camping vehicle or trailer? We found that our four-seater table will fit neatly into the bottom of the Fiesta's hatchback.

What about the height of the table? One of the small, short-legged coffee variety might be suitable. So much will depend on age of children, your family's needs and space available. The table can also be used for cooking on a one- or two-burner stove. If it's taken inside the tent make sure the cooker flames can't touch the walls. A lid on the two burner can also be used as a windshield or splashback (see Chapter Seven).

Picnic chairs which can be bought at so many outlets are quite inexpensive and very light in weight. Chairs designed especially for camping may cost a little more but they will be more stable and should last longer. For instance the canvas on my Lafuma chair has just ripped after 17 years but one of our light alloy picnic chairs gave up before one holiday was over. The choice is yours. Try to imagine how much time will be spent in the chair. For comfort it's best not to have a bar going from side to side underneath the knees or across the back. Small collapsible stools are also obtainable.

COOL BOXES AND WATER CONTAINERS
A whole range of cool boxes and bags are to be found; there are even portable refrigerators. The bags and boxes will be insulated to a certain extent but it would be dangerous to expect them to work like a home refrigerator. Freezer packs will keep food cool for a time but the warming-up process begins on the outward car journey. Also, the heat in a closed tent on a sunny day has to be experienced to be believed.

Don't let these remarks put you off though. We always use a cool bag or box. You'll need some kind of container for food and drinks and at least an insulated box will keep food fresh for a while and should be insect-proof.

Water carriers

Some campsites offer a re-freezing service for the ice packs. Even better, you may discover a site with small lock up refrigerators rather like rows of safe deposit boxes.

We've found it best to buy fresh food every day, keeping a few tins of corned beef and packets of convenience foods for emergencies - or if there's a take-away use that. A cool spot can often be found by the spare wheel in the car, a good place to keep the butter as long as it's in a tightly closed container.

Water containers come in all shapes and sizes, with and without a tap. As already mentioned it's better to buy two 1 gallon than one 5 gallon,

Cool boxes come in a variety of sizes

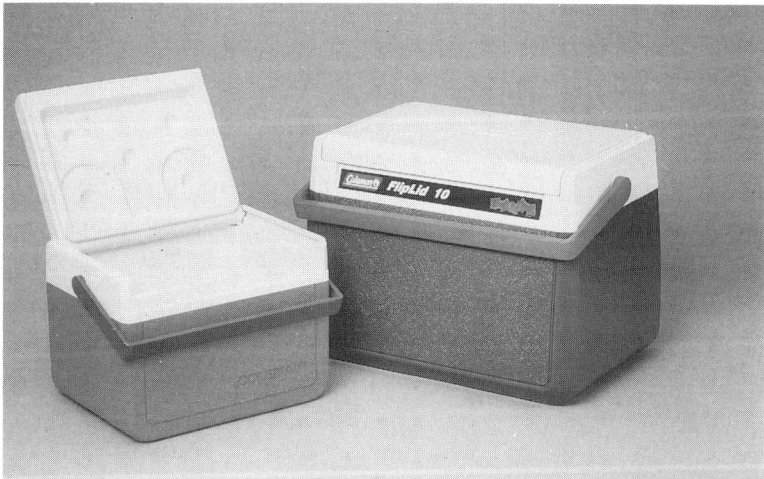

which may be too heavy to carry when full. Simple collapsible or roll-up plastic bag types take up less room than rigid ones. After many years we stick to a straightforward 1 gallon water container with screw cap. We usually go to a site with showers and a washing-up area which means the container is only used for drinking water.

LIGHTING AND HEATING

Two lights are better than one but which to buy? Not all campsites are well lit. You may need a simple torch to see your way across to the loo block as well as a more powerful lamp run by gas or battery. Some models can be connected to the car battery. Gas lights are efficient and quite romantic for sitting outside on a warm continental evening but with children around I feel a battery operated lamp is safer. Some gas containers are disposable and lightweight. The refillable kind cost more to begin with but they are heavier and more stable in use.

Lights which run from the vehicle electrics are of the fluorescent variety and there are some portable fluorescent lanterns run by dry batteries giving off quite a good light. Take your pick. Most campers are tired out after a day in the fresh air. Once the meal has been cooked you may just want to talk by a soft light in which case a good torch or battery lantern might fit the bill.

Likewise you may not need any form of heating, although gas heaters are available. (Follow all the safety rules and don't leave children alone with naked flames.) These can be connected to the same gas container as your light and cooker - one at a time. If this set-up appeals make sure the connections are all compatible.

TOILET AND TOILET TENT

Toilets range from a simple folding potty with disposable liners (available from Boots the Chemist) to flushing, easily emptied Thetford Porta Pottis. Coming somewhere between are the 'bucket and chuck it' Elsans. (See appendix for addresses.) The latter are about half the price of a sophisticated flushing loo. If you've taken the step of buying a trailer for the full set of camping gear there may be space for a toilet and toilet tent. If you plan to take advantage of small minimum facility sites your own loo is more or less essential. Very few supply a WC and if they do there might only be one.

You'll know your children's toilet habits and whether they are past the potty stage. Even if those days are well over try to find room for the potty for night emergencies. If buying a Porta Potti get the right height: there's

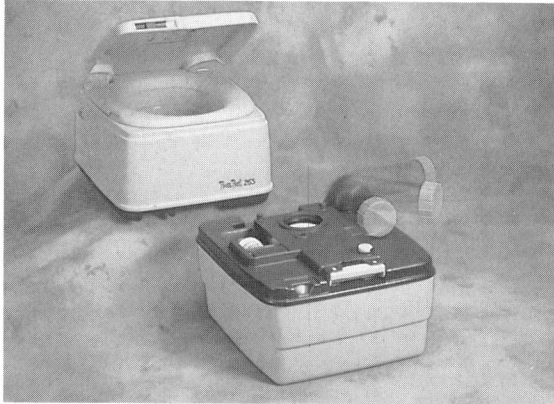

Thetford Porta Potti - one of seven different models

a choice, with seven different models listed.

The difference in the toilet fluids is well worth a mention. Aqua-Kem makes two kinds. The original Aqua-Kem in a blue pack is formaldehyde based and toxic. It is also perfumed, biodegradable and helps dissolve waste matter as well as keeping the holding tank clean. Aqua-Kem Green on the other hand is non-toxic, does not irritate eyes or skin and is, we're told, ecologically and environmentally friendly.

If you're going to buy a toilet tent it might be worth considering one of the double size. The price is not necessarily a lot higher but the extra space could be useful for a wash stand, storing wellingtons and other bits and pieces.

ACCESSORIES

Take a look round your local camping centre or shop, go to one of the 'shops' at an exhibition and you'll enter a camper's Aladdin's cave. The Touchwood Sports catalogue (see appendix for address) is full of little extras that take the 'roughing it' out of camping.

Spare pegs and guylines are not exactly luxury items but the wise camper will remember the Baden Powell motto and 'Be Prepared'. A different type of peg, easier to use, may be discovered. You may want to change to lighter coloured guylines which are brighter to see and not so easily tripped over. You'll find a range of cutlery and cooking sets. A set of nesting saucepans (more in Chapter Seven) take up very little space. Also available is a free-standing wardrobe. There are insulated tea-pots and butter dishes, as well as a pegless clothes line, drying racks, clothes hooks, a tent tidy, you name it. Take as much luxury and comfort as your camping vehicle and pocket will stand.

CHAPTER FIVE
Children's needs

Ask any child if he or she would like to 'go camping' and the answer is almost sure to be an enthusiastic 'yes please, when?'. The excitement of the whole procedure from buying the gear to pegging the last guyline is a never-to-be-forgotten experience.

Recommended child and baby care can change overnight. We do not pretend to be experts in paediatrics. The age at which you should first take youngsters to a holiday in the great outdoors has to be yours or the decision of your medical adviser.

With disposable nappies, food that is simply spooned from a jar and sites with just about every 'mod con', plus playgrounds from simple swings and slides to adventure equipment that would satisfy Tarzan, family camping has never been easier or more rewarding.

SAFETY

In the 1990s we are very safety conscious and you will know your child's needs and habits. Those parents who have themselves camped from an early age may say 'having children won't change things'. True, arriving on site and setting up a tent and equipment will be second nature. Small babies who are breast fed and sleep much of the time will probably cause the least problems. Toddlers who are 'into everything' need to be watched closely, especially when the cooker is alight.

You'll also need to make sure toddlers don't wander off. Even if you've never liked the idea of reins on children, the time may have come when some kind of restraint is necessary: either a harness and reins or one of the 'lead reins', which are two wrist bracelets with a connecting strap.

Shared responsibility is perhaps the name of the game with one partner taking the children off while the other cooks a meal or boils the kettle. Hot drinks can be dangerous if pulled down by a child. At home we are used to putting mugs in a safe place but in unfamiliar surroundings it's so easy to forget.

Sunburn and heatstroke are other hazards. We all know how high the temperature can become in a closed car - a zipped up tent is similar. Take and use sun hats, cover vulnerable arms and legs if youngsters are going to be in the open air for any length of time. The sun doesn't need to be

Harness and reins
from Boots

blazing for any of us to get uncomfortably or even dangerously burnt. Use recommended sunscreen preparations, remembering to re-apply from time to time and especially after swimming.

Everyone in the party needs to be made aware of fire precautions within the 'portable home'. No racing and fooling around, especially when naked flames are about. There's usually a list of fire precautions sewn in to the tent near the kitchen or listed on the erecting instructions. The following are the main points, which of course apply to every camper and not just children.

1. When siting ensure a minimum distance of 6m between adjacent tents or awnings.
2. Do not place cooking, heating or lighting appliances near the sides or the roof.
3. Always observe the safety instructions for these appliances.
4. Never allow children to play near lighted appliances.
5. Keep exits clear.
6. Make sure you know the fire precaution arrangements on the site.

'On site' fire extinguishers or buckets are often kept near the waste bins or water taps. If you want to carry an extinguisher or fire blanket as part of the family's equipment as well as a first aid kit, look in the outdoor catalogues such as the one published by Touchwood Sports of Oxford - or visit your local camping centre.

If camp life is beginning to sound restricting remember hotel and guest house holidays are far from perfect when young children are part of the group. On the whole family camping is relatively free and easy. There's no B&B proprietor to complain if you go back to the accommodation at lunch or any other time of the day. If junior tips his chicken and sweetcorn on the floor or rubs raspberry yogurt in his hair, who will see or care?

Look upon camping as an adventure, with one adult to look after the toddler/s all the time. There will probably be some hiccups, as at home. Note potential hazards and take all necessary precautions.

Two other useful publications with whole ranges of items and clothing that may be suitable for the great outdoors are the Boots *Baby and Child* and the *Mothercare* catalogues. They are both full of information and cost very little (available from larger stores).

It might be worth buying a ready made first aid kit because this will be in a suitable container, although it's usually cheaper to make up your own.

If any of the products are unfamiliar to you, read the instructions before going away and if applicable make sure items are suitable for children. We usually carry first aid items separately from medicines and use two lists which are based on the following. If in doubt ask a qualified pharmacist.

First Aid:

liquid antiseptic	several widths of bandage
triangular bandage	safety pins
plasters	sterile dressings
cotton wool,	tweezers, scissors

(You may have a steel Swiss Army knife which includes these last two. The scissors on my key ring version will cut the corner from an orange container or slice a piece off the plaster strip. You may want to go for the more sterile single packaged plasters.)

'Medicine Chest' - favourite remedies to relieve:

travel sickness	indigestion
headaches	diarrhoea
constipation	sore throat
coughs and colds	toothache
insect bites and stings	sunburn

(and don't forget sunscreen and insect repellent)

If you expect any severe cases of travel sickness see your doctor before leaving home. If anyone in the family has a longstanding illness or is taking medication make sure you ask the doctor's advice before taking off for the campsite. Some medicines have to be kept refrigerated - is there a substitute? Take a small supply of your usual pills and potions, kept in childproof containers and stored in a safe place. If you take a prescription remember that not all chemists stock every item available. You may arrive on a Saturday afternoon and the remedy has to be ordered and won't arrive until Monday morning.

BATHING

Some sites have a parents' room, many don't. You'll even find baths, full and baby size, at some locations. If the site is chosen with care there may be washing cubicles and in most cases hand basins with hot and cold water. The Camping and Caravanning Club is gradually introducing parent and baby rooms as they update their sites and a whole book could be written about campsite showers.

The latter range from the really comfortable with no coin boxes or tokens to worry about to rushing Niagaras falling from a great height to startle small children. Test the shower yourself because they all vary. I'm sure you've already come across the type that is one minute cold and the next treats you like a tomato ready to be skinned. Many parents don't realise just how frightening a strange shower can be to some children.

So much depends on the age, size and mobility of your youngsters. If they are used to a shower then taken calmly there shouldn't be too many problems. If the showers are good and the children old enough the whole experience may be a novelty and you won't be able to keep them out. A large washing up bowl kept especially for body washing purposes can be used for bathing or an 'all over scrub down'.

Most children have become used to public loos in such places as petrol stations. They vary from the excellent to the 'we're not stopping heres'. Many camping sites and parks can be compared to these and the same rules apply. Always be prepared with a toilet roll and possibly soap. I get very cross with the site that has rows of mirrors but doesn't provide soap and/or a hand drier.

Occasionally you'll come across child height wash basins and sometimes there is a minimum age at which children are allowed into the toilet block without an adult. This can be for the benefit of all campers as well as the child because there are small children who just cannot reach the toilet seat without some very unhygienic contortions. If, like the author, you've been a playgroup leader you may know the problems of recently potty weaned toddlers.

Evenflo Disposable bottle and holder

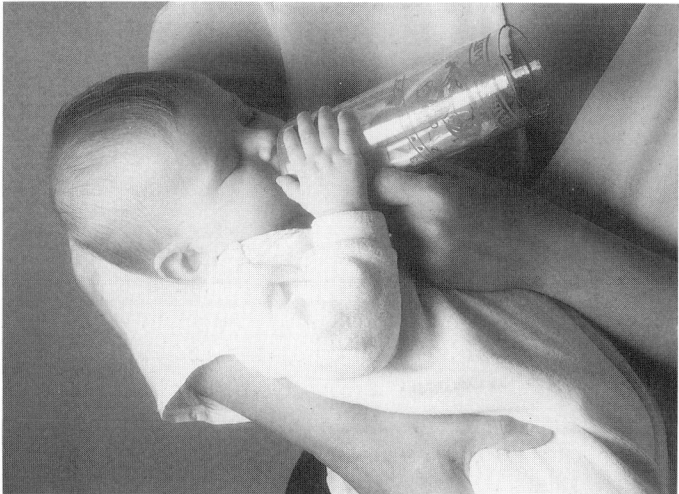

59

FOODS

As with medicines particular milks and baby foods may not always be available when and where you need them, especially abroad. Even within the limited shores of Britain certain brands are not always easy to find. Take a supply. You may believe that 'Breast is Best' in which case most baby feeding aspects will be under control or you will have thought of emergency services. A disposable baby bottle by Evenflo UK sounds interesting. This would mean each feed can start with a new, pre-sterilised bottle. (For address see appendix.)

Research and practise bottle feeding and sterilizing and try any new methods or foods several weeks before the holiday. Babies, toddlers and older children (or their stomachs) may decide they don't like the change. Again this is another advantage of a camping holiday - you can take along favourite foods and drink.

Adults may crave a variety of different meals and thirst quenchers but children usually feel more secure and therefore more relaxed if sticking to the old routine and the brand of wheatibangs they've always eaten. The time for introducing new recipes is not on a camping holiday.

The author is a believer in 'happy parents, happy children' and vice versa. If the children are content, mum and dad are much more likely to enjoy their holiday. This doesn't mean letting the children do what they like, when they think they will, but going along with certain likes and dislikes for a week or so - without them realising.

As with other aspects of child rearing you will have worked out your own meals for toddlers and older children. Just follow the same hygiene rules as you do at home. In fact if it's possible, be even more strict. Make sure hands are washed after every trip to the loo and don't leave any foods uncovered or in warm or hot tents or cars. Leftover foods should not be kept unless you've got a refrigerator - another good reason for taking a 'ready erected' tent or mobile home holiday with proper fridge when the children are small.

For everyone's peace of mind try to keep to similar meal times to those at home. If your children are used to their carers doing a hundred and one things at once and dishing out a quick meal in between cleaning the car and emptying the baby bath - as so many of us do - there may not be any problems but be consistent.

NAPPIES AND POTTIES

What goes into the body needs to be eliminated. Now is the time for my

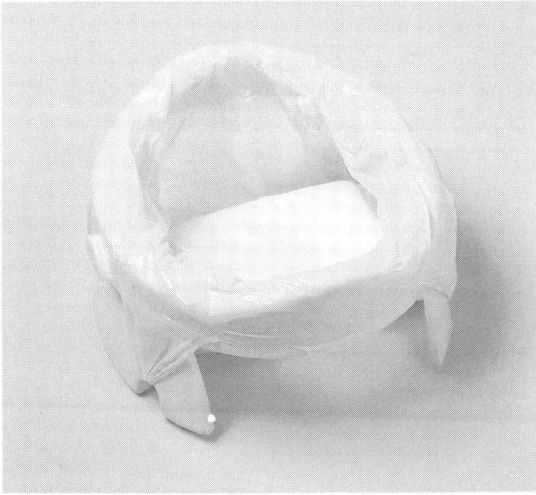

Travelling Potty from Boots

confession. Yours truly put off the first aeroplane flight and the first camping expedition until both of our daughters were out of nappies. Depending on how close they are in ages this time in their lives quickly passes. We all have different stress levels and disposable nappies were only being used by the very rich at that time. Make up your own minds. It may be that you'll try a weekend away as soon as your baby is using a potty during the day and only needs protection at night.

Make sure the potty is a stable one. Grass and groundsheets are not perfectly flat. I'm sure you will have worked out the home toilet procedure and don't need our advice. You'll also need to take your favourite make of nappy, creams and lotions.

Boots markets a handy looking portable travelling potty with disposable pouches - a kind of folding affair with plastic bags to attach. Read the site noticeboard or find out from your site warden or reception just how you should dispose of nappies and other waste.

WHEN, WHERE - THE CAR JOURNEY

In general, parents will be cutting down the mileage once children have arrived on the motoring scene. Presumably the children's car seats and belts will all be in good order. In the early camping days neither children nor parents will be keen on a long drive to the south of France or to Spain, probably in a hot, sticky vehicle.

Most of us will know that sorting out territorial rights on the back seat can start before you've even reached the local petrol station. (It is possible to fly out to the sun for a 'ready erected' tent or caravan holiday.)

Go away for short weekends and settle for a site that is fairly close to home to get used to the outdoor life. For the annual holiday most toddlers will be perfectly happy with a sandy beach and a shallow pool as long as they are close to the family.

Remember that the noise and surge of incoming waves are not only dangerous, they can frighten a two year old who has perhaps never seen the sea before. Our elder daughter screamed louder than the seagulls on her first visit even though she was being carried by dad. We walked away from the waves and all was calm again. Let them get used to this new experience in their own time.

Choose a quiet period, and if school holidays just cannot be avoided try a site away from a popular tourist area if possible (more in Chapter Six).

If you don't feel you've been on holiday without crossing the channel, why not try Brittany, Normandy, Holland or Belgium? Safe, sandy beaches can be found in all these areas and the driving time is not too great. Get in touch with the tourist offices and ask their advice. I won't begin to go into beach pollution. If this aspect worries you there are all kinds of 'best beach' books and leaflets, some quite contradictory. Your local library should be able to help with this type of information.

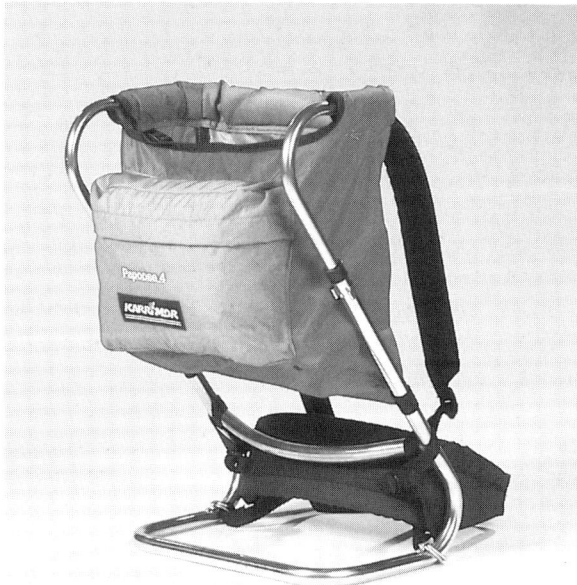

The whole family will begin to work out their own travel pattern.
Karrimor Papoose 4

On short journeys, with frequent stops if necessary, the whole family will begin to work out their own travel pattern.

Depending on ages and different levels of energy this could mean everyone except the driver and possibly navigator goes to sleep. The whole family may take part in car games or each individual could do their own thing such as listening to a personal stereo with story or music tapes.

I'm glad to see that *I Spy* books are still going strong. At around £1 each these are a great idea. (The actual reading part might not be so good if a child is prone to travel sickness. If you expect any severe cases of 'mal de travel' ask your doctor before leaving home.) These little *I Spy* booklets, published by Michelin, include *I Spy on a Car Journey* and *I Spy Inn Signs* and everyone can join in. Points are given for spotting anything from a George and Dragon pub to a radar speed trap. You'll only get four points for noticing the Red Lion but spot a speed trap and a splendid 15 points can be yours. One of the brown caravan park signs gathers 10. *I Spy* badges are given when 1,000 or more in one book have been scored.

I Spy books are also useful 'on site' and during the holiday, for instance *I Spy in the Lake District* has a map and to double the score the owner just answers a series of questions - answers are given at the end of the book. Other titles include *In The Night Sky*, *Wild Flowers*, *In the Country* and *Creepy Crawlies*. All great fun as well as educational.

WET WEATHER

Today's campsites are often equipped with games and TV rooms, cafes and other areas that are under cover. Leaving the site there may be caves to visit, amusement parks with indoor entertainment, or any number of places to get out of the rain. Museums of the '90s for instance are bright with many of them offering 'hands on' experiences for children. It's not advisable to sit about in a damp tent waiting for the sun. Half a day may be bearable but 'get out and about' is my advice.

Again, ages of children might be the deciding factor, and suggestions here could be used for the evenings. During the rest of the year there may be little time for parents and children to get together round the Monopoly or Scrabble boards so wet days on weekends and holidays could be just the time for this kind of family get-together, either using the camping table or going to the leisure room if one is provided. Smaller children may prefer to put a jigsaw puzzle together, perhaps with some help. All kinds of quiz books can be found and a pack of cards for snap and other simple games can go down very well.

Don't forget to take a favourite cuddly toy and other pastimes for the 'littlies'. Older children might enjoy identifying and pressing leaves - if the rain stops long enough to gather them. These can be put between soft toilet paper and even a magazine with a weight on top can do the job unless the leaves are very fleshy. Keeping a holiday diary is another idea, either using a small notebook or buying a special publication often on sale in holiday areas.

The Oxfam *Make-a-Gift* book with over 50 gifts has some very good ideas that could be useful. There's also a series of Letts Pocket Entertainments books written and illustrated as in days gone by - *Conjuring Tricks*, *Parlour Games*, *Fortune Telling* and *Juggling* are the subjects. These are intriguing little books costing under a fiver and as well as giving actual instructions for making things such as a bean bag, the 'olde world' text is quite a laugh.

For instance we learn that 'The dimensions of the bean-bag should be such as is most comfortable to the size of your hand, which will mean that for a cultivated person it will be in the vicinity of 3 inches across, and, for a manual worker or craven, 4 inches across'. They also tell us not to juggle the bean bag higher than one foot above our head, here we could subsitute tent roof where they mention breakable chandeliers!

The Letts company, of course, is also known for its Pocket Guides on subjects ranging from birds and dinosaurs to weather.

CLOTHES FOR CHILDREN

In these times of casual clothes for all occasions, everyday shorts, tee shirts, jeans and a sweater or two with an anorak or warm jacket, preferably of showerproof material, plus a range of underwear will take care of our children's camping wardrobe. This is another advantage of a camping holiday. Denim material takes a long time to dry and is not good for serious walking; polycotton trousers are better. If there's a heatwave swimsuits or trunks will be all that is needed plus a cotton top to cover burnt shoulders. Nights can be cold even in the hottest climates, so be prepared and then relax.

Above: Britain has many excellent sites

Below: Good preparation - sponge off marks

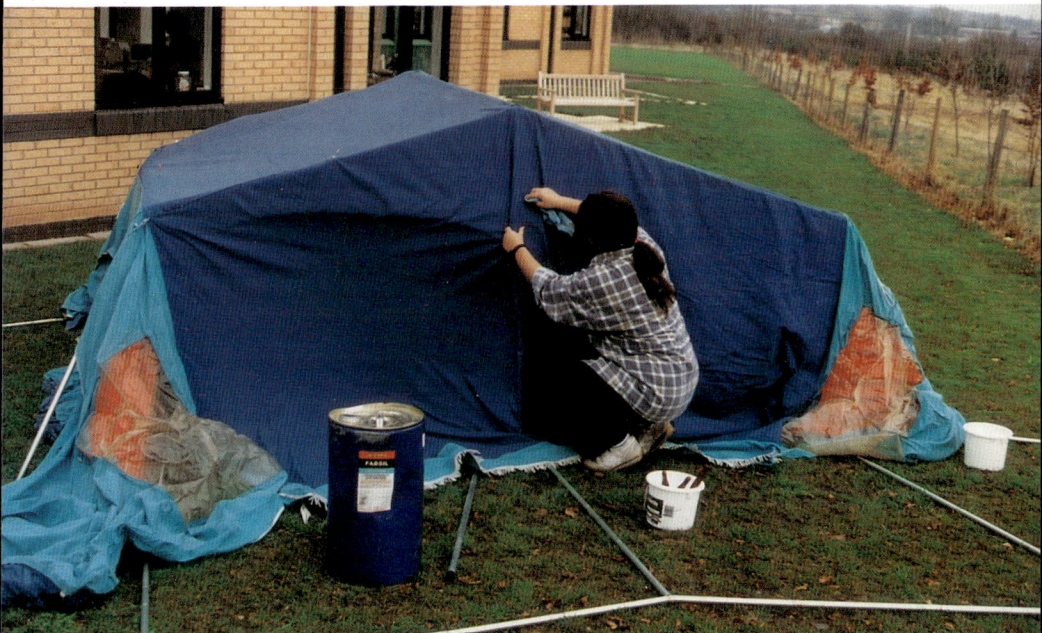

Above:
Improvised cooking on a camp fire needs careful control. Note how the fire is purposely kept small between retaining rocks. Just a few sticks will create enough heat to quickly prepare a meal, then the fire needs to be thoroughly doused. Open fires are banned due to the high risk of conflagration in many countries where summer is tinder dry. The photo above is in Norway where the ground is so damp that there is little danger of fire spreading. *Photo: R.B.Evans*

Right: The joys of lightweight camping are not restricted to summer.
Photo: R.B.Evans

CHAPTER SIX

Pick the Right Site

So you've bought the tent and equipment, now for the spine tingling adventure. The family is 'going camping'. With good planning this could be the start of years of travel abroad, summer holidays spent in tranquil meadows, weekends with club friends - you name it.

To make sure the whole family is going to enjoy this new experience it's essential that careful thought be given to the type of site. Laid back or full of life? Remember those first camping trips are best spent getting to know the tent and equipment. Leave the kyaking or abseiling excursions until day to day living has been sorted out.

So much will depend on the ages and interests of your children. Imagine the worries with a toddler if there's a river or main road close by. Even if you've never believed in reins or a play pen the time to buy one may have arrived. Older children won't thank you for showing them nothing but a wide open field and telling them to enjoy it. Running about may throw off some of their exuberance in the first hour or two but what then? You know your offspring and their personalities, it's impossible to generalize - just remember to give the location some thought.

If you like the sound of being able to turn in for the night after an evening spent sipping the local brews, what about one of the many minimum facility pub sites? Take note of the loos available - some pubs provide 24 hour toilets, at others you need to go armed with your own chemical toilet because the pub doors are closed out of licensing hours.

One little beauty of a site in the Bedfordshire area, with use of a swimming pool during the season and listed by The Camping and Caravanning Club, is run by Ray and Sheila Salt at Great Gransden. Another small site not too far from the A1 is Lodge Farm at Sawtry, between Peterborough and Huntingdon in Cambridgeshire. Own sanitation is essential but if you want to be truly 'away from it all' the latter is the place to pitch your tent and fees are very reasonable.

So how are you to find this perfect site for your family? Once you're 'into' the camping scene one of the best methods is by word of mouth. Get talking to your neighbours, visit the games room or launderette. Not only do friendships start in these places but all kinds of information can be gleaned. 'Don't go to this or that site, the showers are awful' and so on. It's best not to get too carried away with this way of determining which sites are tops. One person's idea of perfection may be another's nightmare. If clean toilets are your first priority ask about these; if you want plenty for the children to enjoy, research that aspect.

At the very start you'll need a good sites guide or list which should be studied before the trip - even if you are not booking in advance. This may seem an obvious step but in the excitement can easily be forgotten until the children have asked for the fiftieth time 'are we nearly there?' and are threatening a wet seat.

The newsagents and bookshop shelves are rich with sites guides of all kinds. A range of ticks, stars and pennants are used for classification which are an excellent indication of what to expect but are not foolproof. They

Visit the laundry room

Choose a good sites guide

may tell you there are hot showers and a swimming pool but symbols do not always reflect the quality.

The AA and the RAC publish comprehensive lists with a separate edition for Europe. Maps are included in each and the AA also gives more localised 'how to get there' diagrams. Both provide written 'how to get there' directions. Entries in the RAC *Camping and Caravanning Guide* - Great Britain and Ireland - are divided into RAC 'Listed' which 'have all the necessary facilities' and 'Appointed' sites which have 'a large number of amenities and superior facilities'. A page of the RAC's requirements for their listed sites is also given.

The AA's *Camping and Caravanning in Britain* classifies those listed by giving each establishment from one to five pennants. You'll also find an explanation of the AA's requirements. There are chapters on a variety of camping and caravanning topics in both the AA and RAC guides.

The English, Scottish and Welsh Tourist Boards publish sites lists as well as the Regional Tourist Boards - Cumbria, West Country, Northumbria etc. (for addresses see appendix). For more local information, tourist information centres (TICs) will usually supply a pamphlet with notes on perhaps as few as a dozen sites in their area.

The Camping and Caravanning Club (the only national Club in Britain for tent campers) issue two guides free to members. One called *Your Big Sites Book* is packed with nearly 5,000 sites from the smallest to the largest and is accompanied by an Ordnance Survey map to pinpoint them. These establishments are not especially recommended by the Club although if a sites liaison officer has been on a visit during the previous year this is noted.

Your Big Sites Book also includes hundreds of minimum facility 'Certificated Sites'. These are small sites for members only which are allowed to take 5 caravans plus a number of tents. Usually in pretty locations they may have just a water tap and a point for emptying chemical toilets which means you do need to take your own loo and toilet tent.

The other Camping and Carvanninng Club sites list, *Your Place in the Country*, is a guide to the 80 or so sites owned or managed by the Club. Wardens are appointed and the sites are inspected and recommended by the Club. This is a more detailed publication in full colour with a page and a sketch map for each site. The map takes you right to the front gate and ideas for 'what to see' in the area are also given.

It's worth pointing out that because of certain plannning requirements some Club Sites accept non-members, so if you haven't signed up don't let that stop you just rolling up if you see one of their green and red signs. Site fees are lower for members and you may decide it will pay you to join there and then.

Alan Roger's 'Good Camps' guides with details of 'Selected Quality' sites were our 'bibles' when our children were young. These are available in separate editions for Britain, France and Europe and each is divided into areas. The latest from the Alan Rogers stable is *Camping and Caravanning - All Year Round - Britain and Europe*.

If a site is only 'satisfactory' the Alan Rogers team will say so. If the loo block is small it will be mentioned. If they didn't like the look of a site or haven't got round to visiting an area these won't be included at all.

The guide tells if locations are lakeside, seaside, or will say if there are comprehensive amenities. There will be a list of exactly what the site has to offer plus distance to beach and into town, how to find it, charges and reservations. After visiting several sites listed in the Alan Rogers guide we agreed with every word of the reports and felt confident that the compilers had the same tastes as us. Other useful sections in the book include lists of 'dogless', 'winter sports' and 'open all year' sites.

'The Best of British' is a group of sites, with their own booklet, which offer better than average facilities and locations. In France the chain to look out for is 'Castels and Camping Caravaning'. Whichever guide you use read the explanation of the symbols at the front of the book.

We've mentioned the location and a few other points to look for when choosing a site. As far as 'on site' facilities are concerned some toilet blocks are beginning to look like first class hotels with dressing tables, trendy lighting and hair care centres. At one time it was said that British sites couldn't compete with those in Europe - and perhaps because a number of continental sites offered a whole range of take-aways, showers, even footbaths this was true.

All this has changed and Britain can hold its head up high with many of its sites offering tiled showers, cubicled wash basins, swimming pools, games and TV rooms as well as launderettes, shops, and salad cleaning and washing-up areas. In fact as much or as little luxury as you like.

Of course the more facilities introduced the higher the fees are going to be. Decisions again. Are we happy to enjoy the great outdoors with a bit of mud on our legs for a nominal fee or do we only feel comfortable if there is soap and paper towels with showers and private cubicles for personal washing - when site fees can cost twice or even three times as much? Thank goodness we have this wonderful freedom of choice. There are many camping sites which come somewhere between these two extremes. Those of us who look for nothing more than well-spaced pitches and a good clean toilet block with hot showers are well catered for.

Camping will cost less if you stick to the Low Season, usually before Easter and from mid-September. Bank Holidays are often classed as High Season. Fees may be on a 'per pitch' basis which includes tent and car, which may or may not include two persons with a charge for extra occupants. It's difficult to compare prices because some may be worked out 'per person' from the start. A small fee is usually charged for children over 5 years and dogs. In 1993 The Camping and Caravanning Club were offering special family rates - more in Chapter Eleven.

If taking young children and going away for a week or more you'll need a laundry room, with a washing machine and spin or tumble drier if my guess is right. Some so-called 'laundries' only have a deep sink. Check before booking. The toilets will need to be acceptable and if you're going abroad with youngsters make sure the site has some 'British style' loos. Don't let campers' tales of 'loos abroad' put you off. This is where research will pay. We've recently been to a site in France which had a gleaming array of our style toilets, plus an adjoining section with cubicles containing a bidet and a hand-basin - all kept spotlessly clean.

Always take a toilet roll. Even at some of the higher priced sites proprietors seem to think these are unnecessary - or may provide the hard and glossy kind.

Looking back 25 years I think my husband and I should have been prosecuted for cruelty, carting our young daughters to a truly rural site abroad where the only toilets were 'squat down' and smelt worse than the farmyard itself. Some of these hole-in-the-ground WCs are very clean and can be even more hygenic than the 'sit upons'. Perfectly acceptable if in fact you can squat down. Certain disabilities just will not allow this and cramp in the legs, as occasionally suffered by people like the author, are also a bit of a nuisance even if hilarious when the results are recounted over a glass of wine.

Incidentally, if you arrive at a campsite on the continent and find squat down loos, take a look in each cubicle, you may find half or more of them contain 'uprights'. And while we're talking on many campers' favourite topic, in Finland we found some beauties at a camping site/sports centre with toilet, hand-basin, mirror, in fact a self-contained bathroom in each compartment. The complaints we've had from some men is that the architects tend to forget that men also like to wash in a cubicle as much as we womenfolk.

Are your children used to taking a shower? Some of these are excellent, especially when no coins are involved (more in Chapter Five). You may have to change coins into tokens at the reception desk or showers could be free. At a few sites there might be a full size bath and/or a child care room with baby bath but these are not as numerous as many of us would like. Our family used to take an extra large washing-up bowl which served very well for a children's stand-up wash or you may want to take your baby bath from home. However, as the amount of equipment you'd like to take begins to need a double decker bus, decisions on just where to stop have to be made.

To book or not to book a chosen camping site is a major question? For some families, especially if children are old enough to enjoy the whole adventure, the 'freedom' aspect means just packing the car and taking off when the weather and mood dictates. That can work if you don't mind a few surprises. The traffic is heavy, it's getting dark and the sites are all full because the current heatwave means every other camping family is heading for that cool patch of grass next to a river. Give the site a ring before leaving home.

In the main it is advisable to book for Bank Holidays, especially the Spring Bank Holiday break, as well as for the July and August school holidays. Most parents of toddlers will be looking for a sandy beach. This means that sites close to the coast at the busy times will quickly fill up and might be booked months in advance. Mind you, it's often possible to find a quiet, well run site a little inland where the family may be a lot happier - without booking.

If your children are under school age why not try late May or June for a holiday before the schools break up, or September/October when older children are back at their desks. The weather in early autumn can be especially good for walking and other activities. Tire the family out and they won't mind how early it gets dark! If camping at either end of the season and taking off 'on spec' make sure the site will be open. A few stay open year round. Sites run by The Camping and Caravanning Club vary in their opening dates. Chertsey is open all year, one or two open in February, others not until the end of March. Some close at the end of September, others not until 1st November.

On a first ever camping trip arriving on site can be quite daunting. The reception area may be like the foyer of a cinema, or the cash could be paid over the kitchen table at a farmhouse. There may be no-one on duty at all with a notice saying 'someone will be round to collect fees in the morning'. Take things quietly, park and have a look round before you pitch. Any site worth staying at won't mind if you walk into the loo block or check out any other facility, though it's wise to park in the designated spot and ask first.

You may be given a form to fill out, name, address, car registration, number of nights and how many people. On the continent you may be asked for a Camping Carnet (more in Chapter Nine) as well as where you've travelled from and destination when leaving. There may be 'minimum stay' rules, sometimes 3 days; there can be a reduction for longer visits.

At a smaller site picking a pitch or space to erect your tent may be left to you. Choose a level spot, not under trees as if the weather is wet the dripping carries on for ages and some leaves give off a sticky substance. Of course in hot countries you'll be pleased to have some shade. If everything is really organised there will be a plan of the site with a cross marking the numbered spot. The Warden or one of his assistants may lead you round by bicycle and point out the washing-up area, toilet block and any other amenities. Drive or walk round - and don't be rushed. If the pitch is not up to scratch ask for another - there's no way the Warden will know your preferences. Some campers ask for a pitch as near to the wash area as possible, others like to stay at a distance from this busy centre.

If it's late afternoon when most people are just arriving and the reception staff are up to their eyes in paperwork, being choosy is not so easy. On that first day try to arrive before the evening rush. We also find that during busy weeks the afternoon can be a good time for taking a shower. Try to remember the hour or so that the loo block will be closed for cleaning. You won't be able to shower then but generally there will be a toilet open, possibly the disabled room.

In the main the more informal the site the fewer the rules. Dogs may or may not be accepted. Everyday courtesy is expected, for instance no noise between 10pm and 7.30am. Personal stereos and ear pieces are a great idea, as the noise of a radio seems to get louder as it moves through the walls of a tent. No dogs should be running loose. On the other hand never leave pets or children in a closed tent as heat can build up similar to that in a car left in the sun.

There may be a reminder of rules on the site information board. For instance where to dispose of waste water and rubbish. Occasionally young children are not allowed to visit the toilets un-accompanied. If barbecues are permitted make sure the initial smoke doesn't choke your neighbour. After all, if we all went mad on the freedom bit, breaking all the rules and letting our children kick their football close to tents and caravans, everyone else's holiday could be spoilt. That would finish off their freedom to enjoy.

If the pitches aren't numbered or marked don't set up home too close to another unit. Your family may not worry too much about privacy but if there's a large meadow take advantage of it and spread out. Some campers seem to like their guylines to be friendly with their neighbours, overlapping even. Most of us will frown or let you know this closeness is not appreciated - for fire safety if for no other reason.

As we've said previously, just use common sense and courtesy. Camping is only one form of everyday living and for all ages. Just relax and enjoy the excitement and any adventures that happen along the way.

CHAPTER SEVEN
The camp kitchen

Convenience and take-away foods have revolutionised the camping scene. Very few people expect the traditional carefully prepared meat, two veg and a pudding these days. Healthy eating luckily includes salads and fruit which are just right for the outdoor life, with no cooking required. However, the camp kitchen is far from redundant. Everyone knows that active holidays and ravenous appetites go together like bangers and beans. Imagine life out-of-doors with no heady aroma of bacon frying.

Even if the family only uses a tent for bed and breakfast you'll need to boil a kettle for tea or coffee and then there's toast for breakfast.

Quickly prepared foods are great if the tent is just used for overnight accommodation, perhaps at weekends. If the family is taking off hang gliding or cycling for instance, they may pack a picnic and eat out in the evening. If the whole point of a camping trip is to relax and enjoy living out of doors to the full then cooking and eating is an important part of the holiday and once children are over any faddy stage you may want to try out all kinds of recipes.

Forget chasing off to the nearest theme park where the meal will probably be lost on a white knuckle ride anyway. Getting back to a more laid back way of life is what many of us crave. Experimenting with sea foods fresh from the net, accompanied by local produce bought from a roadside stall or a Pick Your Own field, are all part of this philosophy.

Mix a few instant foods with traditional fruit and vegetables and the balance between quick and easy and healthy can't be bad. Sensible eating is my phrase for the combination.

The style of kitchen unit and cooking stove you choose will tie in with this wide variety of reasons for setting up home in a meadow - as well as the size and design of tent. More questions to be asked here. How much cooking do you intend to do? Will it be of the experimental type or conventional meals, both of which need a two burner? Maybe you'll be eating out or using take-aways with just the occasional quick and easily put together tent meal. How many people will be 'eating in'? Do you need two burners and a grill? Does your tent have a kitchen annexe - will there be space for a full size kitchen unit?

It's possible to buy stoves that run on petrol, paraffin and methylated spirit but the most convenient and widely used fuel for family campers is liquid petroleum gas or lpg, either butane, propane or a mixture of the two. The family camper is likely to be visiting Britain and Europe where the lpg gas is to be found in quite out of the way places. If you have your sights on third world countries a petrol or paraffin stove may be preferable and it's worth knowing that in very low temperatures the butane/propane mix may be the best choice.

For comfort and safety a kitchen unit with a windshield and several shelves for storing provisions is the most popular - the two burner stove is positioned on the top layer. Relatively light in weight these units can include a hanging larder with a zipped net door panel, a plate rack, extra clip-on shelves and there may be a cut-out section for a washing-up bowl. This may sound as though you'll need a pantechnicon to hold all the 'mod cons' but a camping kitchen can be folded down into a flat package for transportation.

A windshield serves more than one purpose. Yes, it will keep draughts away from the two burner and help to boil the kettle quicker as well as making for more efficient and consistent cooking. From a safety point of view a windshield should also stop any draughts blowing the cooker flames onto the tent wall. Canvas can catch fire very quickly. A windshield will also keep fat and other cooking splashes from spoiling the tent fabric. Oily marks are not only unsightly but are also very difficult if not impossible to remove.

An out-of-doors barbecue is another option for the evening meal - either charcoal or gas operated, but this is usually an addition to everyday kitchen equipment. To be recommended because the men of the tent are inclined to take over! One of the low, compact, hibachi barbecues which we've found large enough for four will pack away into quite a small space. Disposable barbecues can also be found. A couple of words of warning though: find out if the site allows barbecues and don't smoke out your neighbours.

When it comes to the actual cooker the most popular choice is a double burner with grill. As mentioned there should be a windshield of some kind. If one is fitted to your kitchen unit make sure the cover of the two burner is not on hinges and can be completely removed. Most double burners fold down to a certain extent. Check the size before deciding.

Another point to look out for is the type of grill. Will it be capable of toasting two slices of bread at once? Some only take one and it could be

Grillogaz Nouveau

lunch time before breakfast is served. Safety taps and a simmering facility are also important features. Gone are the days when the cooker roared away and frizzled up the sausages on the outside leaving the inside raw.

The Grillogaz Nouveau (Camping Gaz) which also has side windshields and a grill pan is one example of the 'complete' cooker. This runs off a 907 cylinder which we've found is quite sufficient for a family of four for a two week holiday. The great thing about Camping Gaz is that refills are available at so many different outlets and in most countries of the world.

If you've decided to go in for fairly lightweight camping and are counting the cost, do you need a grill? A single or double burner that fits directly onto the gas cylinder might be suitable. The Camping Gaz Service Plus, a two burner which screws directly onto a cylinder, operates for 27 hours on a 907 and 18 hours on the smaller 904. Windshields are sold separately.

When on my solo car lightweight trips using a high dome polyester tent I take a Camping Gaz Carena single burner and a 907 container. The larger container is more economical and gives some extra height to the cooker. A good point if you like to cook in more comfort while sitting in a camping chair. The 907 can also be used for a gas lantern in the evening.

COOKWARE - CUTLERY - TABLEWARE

The amount and type of saucepans will again depend on number of campers in the party and how much cooking will take place. One of the sets or canteens are preferable - I like non-stick, again a personal choice. Along with kitchen roll to mop up, non-stick pans have taken a lot of work out of camp cookery.

A canteen will usually contain several saucepans, for instance a 9in dia stewpan, an 8in saucepan plus a milk pan and a deepish lid that can be used for frying. For transportation these sit one inside the other and the lid is secured by a strap. Very neat and will pack away into a small space.

Although it is possible to take cooking pans from the home kitchen there are a couple of drawbacks and both could be safety hazards. One is the fixed handle. Campsite cookery is a scaled down process unless you're going in for large numbers as with scout and guide groups. If your cooker has windshields there may not be space for handles to be turned round to the side in a safe position.

The other is the fact that a home saucepan for 6 people may have a wide base rather than being deep like the canteen version designd for a two burner stove. One regular saucepan may take up too much cooker space. Camping saucepans have a detachable handle which is not only useful from a packing point of view but it means there is no handle to stick out when cooking is taking place. Some are supplied with one handle, others with two and a separate grip can be bought to fit cooking utensils with the beaded type of rim.

The dry cooking pan and pressure cooker are other options for providing a hot meal. If you're well used to a favourite pressure cooker why not try it out on a camping trip. Advertisements for dry cookers are to be found in most camping and caravanning publications but as yet the author has not tested one. A folding oven is another 'luxury' I've tended to keep away from but the Coleman company makes one - with a shelf - which folds down flat and can be used over a single burner. Great stuff for the dedicated cook.

A kettle and a teapot are other pieces of gear that some campers cannot manage without. A kettle is usually quicker and safer than a saucepan for boiling water. If you only use a tea bag in a mug at home it's highly unlikely that you'll buy a teapot for camping but again a single teapot could be safer

Cookware

than four or five mugs with boiling water in them. Just make sure you keep any hot water away from children.

Whether you take cutlery and tableware from home is yet another decision. Knives and forks may get lost, thrown out with the dirty water, used in the sand pit or whatever, so don't take the heirloom silver. Many of us start off with cheap and cheerful plastic plates and mugs. They won't break the bank and yet will do the job successfully. On the other hand there are some really stylish melamine crockery sets on the market. These are light in weight and give the camping trip a much more luxurious feel. If you buy the plastic to start it might last for years and you could be sorry the cash wasn't splashed out for melamine in the first place.

If staining occurs on the plastic or melamine cups there are several remedies. A special product is available but we have used baby's bottle fluid and I'm told denture cleaner does the same job. These products may also come in handy to clean out a water container that hasn't been dried out thoroughly after a camping trip.

Take one mug or cup, knife, fork, spoon and teaspoon for each person but also carry extras for cooking as well as losses. Don't go through the trauma of withdrawal symptoms if you have a favourite kitchen knife, potato peeler or cheese grater and the like. Either take these essentials along or buy a set that is equally as efficient. There are times when 'making do' is just not good enough and hassle free camping should always be uppermost in our minds.

Other 'essentials' for me are a good bread knife, tin opener, cork remover, kitchen roll and plastic sandwich bags. The latter can be used for their intended purpose as well as anything from holding leaves for pressing to rubbish bags in the car.

A certain amount of 'sealing lid' food containers will be needed, to keep ants out of the sugar for instance. In fact all food needs to be enclosed. Creepy crawlies can send out 'come and get it' messages over an amazing distance. Tupperware is a part of most of our lives and there are stacks of other containers that can be tightly closed.

A whole range of jars and boxes can be taken from home and many campers all year round go to great lengths to find products that are sold in strong screw topped jars or containers. Our day-to-day sugar is kept in a small screw topped jar that once held mint sauce - to be refilled from the sugar bag when necessary. We use very little sugar these days and the opened bag with the top folded over is kept in a Tupperware storer alongside the corn flakes in their waxed inner bag.

You'll work out a way of doing things. You may want to transfer everything, including jam, tidily to a set of plastic containers before leaving home. The foregoing is to give an idea of what can be done. Re-using kitchen jars has to be recycling at its best and you may never again buy a pot of marmalade without looking at its potential! A few words of warning. Remember glass is breakable and heavier than plastic and the lightweight plastic bottles as used for squashes do not take kindly to being re-used - they can suddenly leak from an innocent looking crease.

Other essentials for me these days are a couple of screw top containers to take the remainder of the orange juice that comes in a waxed box. If you've cut off the corner and haven't used much there could be spillage when moving to the next site. Buying the small juice packs is probably a better idea because orange and other juices can go off in a hot tent the same as other consumable products.

Make sure all food and drink containers are kept scrupulously clean and only use wide necked bottles that can be more easily cleaned. Don't throw away the baby's bottle brush. Use all the same hygiene rules as you would at home, not forgetting that ice boxes and picnic bags are not refrigerators and will only keep food cold for a limited length of time. Even so, at least one is indispensable.

FEEDING THE FAMILY

At one time campers and caravanners would load up enough tins and packets of convenience foods to stock a mini-market, especially if travelling to the continent. A levelling off of many food prices between Britain and Europe and self-service shops, where no translations are necessary, make this process less important. On the other hand picking up a tin or two and a few packets on the weekly shopping run can spread out both the cost and the enjoyment of a holiday.

Shopaholics will quickly say 'But isn't that what travelling is all about, finding out just what is available in other parts of the country/world?' If this is the case and/or car space is at a premium just take enough food for a day or so. Again it's horses for courses and I suppose we should discuss the difference between the holidaymaker and the traveller. Most campers have a sense of adventure and not many of us can afford to travel full-time. This means our breaks from work have to serve as part holiday relaxation and part travel when we like to delve into the history and everyday life of a country or area.

As a dedicated walker and photographer I spend as little time as possible at the supermarket shelves. It's less effort for me to chase around my local shop where I can easily pinpoint the goods needed for a camping trip. On the other hand when the car is going to be full of people we tend to stick to emergency rations only. Vestas, a couple of tins of corned beef (I wish a less dangerous method of opening would be invented), some pasta, either canned or in a packet. Also on this list is a packet of cream crackers and a box of triangular cheeses.

So let's start with food for the journey. Nothing chocolatey, sticky or fatty for children, especially if car sickness is likely to be a problem. Fizzy drinks are not a good idea either. If this is to be a 'first-ever' holiday camping trip first go away for weekends and try a few picnics to get an idea of what might be needed.

Straightforward sandwiches with fillings that don't easily fall out are a good idea. Other people like to take individual Tupperware containers with bite sized pieces of salad - you may like to carry both. Vegetarians will have their own ideas and recipes. Cooked ham or a quiche of some kind as well as pork pies are usually popular if you can keep them cool and there are no diet limitations. Apples and cucumber are other fairly clean additions. I like to eat a tomato with my lunch but as these are inclined to squirt every which way they are perhaps not so suitable for a journey.

At this point I must mention that 'handiwipes' and tissues should always be carried in a door pocket or similar easily accessible position. Toilet roll, soap and towel should also be packed near the top. They may be needed at a service station and if there's water in your camping container it's always possible to freshen up along the way.

Arriving on site and erecting the tent can be quite hectic. Convenience foods then come into their own but can be quite expensive when catering for a family of four. Most are sold in two person quantities. However to save cash it's possible to use one packet plus extra rice, pasta or a good crusty loaf. You'll know your family's appetites. All kinds of fruit and salads or frozen vegetables can accompany these quick dinners.

One of our most memorable meals was eaten at a chateau site in France. After travelling all day and setting up our frame tent we were hungry and exhausted with only a tin of corned beef and two-day old bread to look forward to. The restaurant was closed but a take-away could offer us mounds of pommes frites. In minutes we were tucking in to chips, corned beef, pickles we'd discovered at the bottom of a box and a bottle of wine. Truly an al fresco banquet.

Most of the larger sites and even quite small ones have a freezer cabinet and also sell bread, milk, eggs, bacon and other basic foods, enough to prepare a meal without too much hassle. Eating habits have changed dramatically in the last few years and many of us have given up baking cakes - that is apart from when going on a camping trip. Those expensive iced fancies in the supermarket are all very well for a dainty afternoon tea and perhaps children who need coaxing. Most campers will want to eat something more satisfying like good old-fashioned fruit cake.

If you've got time and inclination by all means bake the traditional large fruit cake which will be welcomed at all times of the day. I go for the individual rock cake variety. Admittedly not as scrumptious as 'cut and come again' cake but they are quicker to cook and there's no dirty knife when eating in the great outdoors.

We've given ideas for the journey and for a first evening meal, now come the other dishes. Easily prepared foods such as soup mixes, instant mashed potato, savoury rice, soya-based vegeburgers and pastas are all very useful. Most can be obtained on the continent but will you be able to understand the directions. Do you have a measuring/mixing jug? Have a look round your local supermarket as there are so many one pot snacks, instant custards and quick-dried vegetables. Look for pasta and rice that is really 'quick cook' - they do vary by a few minutes. It's also possible to buy 'ready meals' such as 'Wayfarer' from camping shops, some of which

Left:
Perfect camping by a clear running stream in the breathtaking surroundings of Switzerland's Ticino Alps. Some people thin`; lightweight camping is the best of all, but it requires effort to reap the rewards.
Photo: R.B.Evans

Right:
Sun, sand and a river close by - a great recipe for a successful family camping holiday. This is in the very popular Ardèche gorges of France.
Photo: R.B.Evans

A combination of camping and walking gives teenagers a useful outlet for
their energies and often instils a lifelong love of the outdoors.
This idyllic scene is in the Grimsel valley of Switzerland
Photo: R.B.Evans

Stainless steel flasks

are easy to prepare and delicious but they tend to be fairly expensive for a family.

We don't propose to go into conventional meals and cookery as readers will have their own favourites. The idea is to point out that there is no need for anyone to spend hours over the two burner to produce nutritious, satisfying meals. Freedom of choice with a bit of forward planning is what it's all about. If you're experimenting with recipes and local produce don't forget to send me an invitation - I'll bring a bottle!

All kinds of free leaflets are available from the Batchelors Nutritional Advice Centre (see appendix for address). These include different ways of using savoury rice, pasta, and noodles as well as soups and 'Beanfeast', which is a soya mince product with a good shelf life. Some recipes are not suitable for the two burner but my goodness they are all making me drool with their great ideas.

Which brings me to drinks. Well, what is your usual tipple? Children have their own likes and dislikes. Cans of fizzy drink can be a nuisance, one careless squirt and clothes, windows and steering wheel could be sticky for the rest of the holiday. Ready made up squash in a proper container is a good idea, and individual waxed cartons, although the latter are not always foolproof. Pure fruit juices can upset the stomachs of small children - those labelled 'fruit drinks' are usually less scouring. If taking a training mug test to see if it is leakproof, not all are.

Our family rule states that no alcohol is to be consumed until the tent has been erected. The driver has to stay on the soft drinks as does the navigator if you want to keep on the correct route. Let everyone wait. Alcohol is not good for tolerance and temper anyway. Never forget a supply of plain water as sometimes this is the only acceptable drink.

Even if life seems impossible without a cup of tea or coffee it's unlikely you'll want to stop for a fresh brew up on the camping stove. There are some very good stainless steel vacuum flasks on the market. They won't break but the large size will be heavy if you're hoping it can also be used for the rucksack.

If you decide to use a thermos don't add the milk but take a fresh supply or use the dried variety. Depending on where your journey takes you a motorway service station could be just what is needed for everyone's sanity. Some families find that daylight journeys with frequent stops keep children and parents at their happiest, others set off during darkness and tuck the kids down to sleep the time away.

CHAPTER EIGHT
Camping in Britain

The venue of that first ever camping holiday will mainly depend on your home location. There's not a lot of point in driving scores of miles if the time will be spent on site sorting out the tent and equipment. If you've bought a frame tent, kitchen unit and a full range of gear a little practice helps. Take it easy.

If the choice has been a lightweight or touring outfit it's possible that the trial run can take place in the garden although that won't give a true picture of the great outdoors. The more adventurous will want to take off to an area they've had their eye on, sometimes for years.

We've covered how to pick a site in Chapter Six; this particular section is about 'where to go'. Most of us will know about the popular holiday areas. Dozens of excellent camping and caravanning parks can be found in the West Country, especially Devon and Cornwall. The Isle of Wight has a good supply, as well as the Lake District, Peak District, Somerset, Yorkshire and Humberside and East Anglia - and generalizing even more, Wales, Scotland and Ireland.

The Camping and Caravanning Club 'Sitefinder Map' which is printed by Ordnance Survey is excellent in highlighting National Parks and Areas of Outstanding Natural Beauty as well as pinpointing Club and other camp sites. If you can't make up your mind where to head for just spread out a map. Don't be misled though, the hidden corners might be outside those tantalising stretches coloured in green. It's difficult to win; there are few lavishly equipped camping and caravan sites in the hidden haunts of our beautiful country.

This is a quick round-up of holiday suggestions concentrating on impressive places we've visited. We'll be unpopular in some quarters if an area is missed out, but this doesn't mean it is not worth visiting - we just haven't been there - yet.

Be adventurous and search out a lesser known place to pitch. Look for a cycle hire organisation, an activity or craft centre that is not highly advertised. Do some research, read magazines and books, watch TV holiday programmes and compare recommended sites with tourist board literature. Discover your own favourite camping spot and you could find that keeping it to yourself might be the best policy - otherwise the 'site full' board may be out next time! Some districts may overlap. For Tourist Board addresses see appendix.

ENGLAND

Cumbria

Let's try and keep to alphabetical order and begin with Cumbria or the Lake District. What can we note that hasn't already been written? Lakes and mountains stretching over its 880 square miles. Although this is England's most visited National Park a walk outside peak times will bring you to some peaceful spots. Wordsworth, Coleridge and Southey were all inspired by the landscapes.

Skiddaw is an example of the more rounded hills, Scafell and Helvellyn are rugged. Always remember that the weather can change extremely quickly. Take food and drink, wet weather gear, a warm sweater, wear good shoes or boots and carry a map and compass if you want to 'get away from it all'. Stick to distances within the party's capabilities.

Lake Windermere is a popular spot. The roads can be crowded at peak times but the visitor will soon see why so many people do drive along its banks and wander around the souvenir shops. Some of the best walks are on the west shore and to get a good impression of the area, go on a steamer trip.

In direct contrast Ennerdale Water is the only lake without a public road along its shore. It's a bit less 'chocolate boxy' than Windermere and the Forestry Commission forest offers quiet tracks and trails for walkers. There are very few campsites in this area though; Keswick, Coniston, Ullswater and Windermere are more liberally sprinkled.

The Brockhole National Park Centre just outside Windermere is probably the best place to start if you haven't done much homework. Places to see include Brantwood, Dove Cottage and Rydal Mount.

Before we leave this area I must mention the Settle-Carlisle Railway and the Eden Valley between the Lake District and The Pennines, which is good walking country. This could come under the 'hidden corner' banner. The Wild Rose Caravan and Camping Park at Ormside, Appleby-in-Westmorland, is an excellent site open all year. There's a special field for tenters with mains electric and a separate toilet block. For walks in 'Settle-Carlisle Country' look for a book by Colin Speakman and John Morrison published by Leading Edge Press.

East Anglia

England's seaside resorts have made quite a come-back. Piers are being polished up, new attractions have been added, many of them under cover. If it's fun you're after England can provide it. You'll know your own coastal areas. In eastern England, from Skegness to Southend, just about every type of beach or entertainment can be found.

There are lively theatres in towns like Great Yarmouth, Clacton, Skegness, Hunstanton, Lowestoft and Felixstowe. Southend has some good theme parks for younger children in the shape of Never-Never Land and Peter Pan's Playground while Lowestoft's Pleasurewood Hills, Great Yarmouth's Pleasure Beach, the Oasis Centre at Hunstanton and Butlin's Funcoast World at Skegness are all-weather attractions for all the family.

Living in Bedfordshire our most visited camping areas are in East Anglia, usually the Norfolk coast. Yes, we've bought one of those little saucers of cockles at Southend, eaten Colchester oysters, worked our way around that sticky cotton wool called candy-floss and swooped up down and around every roller coaster we could find.

In a more serious vein nature reserves have been created at many points along the east coast. Lonely Gibraltar Point near Skegness, the Broadlands behind Lowestoft and Great Yarmouth, the Landguard reserve in Felixstowe and the salt marshes and sand dunes of Norfolk for instance.

If we fancy a weekend break, sometimes testing a tent, then the time is spent in-county. The Shuttleworth Collection near Biggleswade with Flying Days during the season is well worth a visit. The Headquarters of the Royal Society for the Protection of Birds at Sandy is another popular day trip; there are plenty of original gift ideas in their shop and several nature walks have been waymarked.

The choice of sites in Bedfordshire is rather limited but there are some excellent minimum facility locations, some on a farm, others in the grounds of a public house. (Other sites can be found in the neighbouring counties of Buckinghamshire, Cambridgeshire, Essex, Hertfordshire, and Northamptonshire - yet more 'undiscovered countryside'.) This is where a bit of research can come in handy. Although quite close to London, East Anglia is one of the most unspoilt regions in England with working farms and thatched cottages as well as quaint fishing villages and medieval towns.

East Midlands - or Middle England

This combination of counties stretches from the golden sand beaches of Lincolnshire through Robin Hood Country to the Derbyshire Peaks and

Dales, to Northamptonshire. You'll find historic houses and castles as well as farm and theme parks. Activity holiday enthusiasts are well catered for in the Peak District with cycling, walking, rock climbing, gliding and hang-gliding.

Between the peaceful Lincolnshire Wolds and the Peak District comes Worksop with nearby Clumber Park (NT). The latter offers 3,800 acres of parkland, an 80 acre lake, cycles for hire, events and exhibitions - plus a campsite. Clumber Park would make a good base for visiting The Sherwood Forest Visitor Centre where you can take a short walk through woodland to see the 500 year old Major Oak, said to have been where Robin Hood was able to hide.

Nottingham itself may need little introduction. The Castle Museum, Museum of Costume and Textiles, Lace Hall and the statue of Robin Hood are all worth seeing. There's plenty of activity at Rutland Water in Leicestershire and Northampton is famous for its shoe making. You'll certainly find picturesque hidden corners in the latter two counties and don't miss Turner's Musical Merry-Go-Round in Northampton, listen to the mighty Wurlitzer, ride on a galloping horse - in fact there's good old fashioned fun for everyone.

Heart of England
From the excellent walking areas of the Cotswolds to bustling Birmingham with its theatres, art galleries - and for chocoholics Cadbury World at Bourneville - there are contrasts to be found in this wide area. In Shakespeare's country and Stratford-upon-Avon you can take an open top bus tour to see the sights.

Over to the Marches and the English/Welsh border and down as far as the Royal Forest of Dean and Stroud in Gloucestershire, this is another area a bit short on the larger type of campsite but you'll find lots of quiet and pretty corners tucked away at either side of the mouth of the Severn. Both the Stroud and the Forest of Dean District Councils publish an excellent tourist guide with details of camping sites as well as suggestions for walks.

Back to our meander around the rest of the Heart of England. Follow the map upwards to Shropshire with the Ironbridge Gorge Museum, then there are the Staffordshire potteries with the Wedgwood Visitor Centre and on to Leek at the edge of the Peak District National Park.

If your addiction is more of the alcoholic type the cider orchards of Hereford and Worcester may be calling and nature lovers won't want to miss The Wildfowl and Wetlands Trust at Slimbridge founded by the late Sir Peter Scott.

London

Where do we start when writing about England's most popular tourist destination? The Tower of London, the River Thames and St Pauls still give me a buzz no matter how many times I gaze at them. Then there's the Covent Garden complex, St Katherine's Dock and on and on. Thorpe Park at Chertsey on the outskirts gets a lot of royal attention and the rides are always being up-dated.

Off peak, out of season is the time to visit London but make sure the attractions you want to see do not shut up shop after the crowds have gone.

Living within easy British Rail distance of the capital we haven't used sites around London but the Camping and Caravanning Club Site at Chertsey, the Caravan Club Sites at Crystal Palace and Abbey Wood are open all year round and open to non-members and tenters. There are train services to central London from quite close to the above sites and Travelcards can be purchased.

Camping sites close to the big city need to be booked in advance during the summer months. We get a lot of visitors from abroad and the pitches soon become full. I believe at Abbey Wood tenters have to take their chance and at Chertsey it may be a case of Members Only during high season, so check first. There are other Club sites close to London that accept non-members, open from around April until October, plus a few privately run establishments.

North West

We could start with Manchester and a ramble along Coronation Street on a Granada Studios Tour, or Blackpool for the ever popular illuminations, or maybe Liverpool to catch that ferry across the Mersey. Then what about Chester for a day of shopping in elegant surroundings with a walk around the city wall.

The North West tourist board region stretches from Nantwich in Cheshire to Morecambe and Lancaster in Lancashire, moving across to Saddleworth and Pennine country. Wigan Pier always sounds like a music-hall joke until you go there. Catch a canal waterbus, with a glass top that reminds you of Amsterdam. See, hear and touch life as it was in 1900; you might even get your knuckles rapped in the schoolroom because professional actors are there to wield the cane.

One excellent site in the North West area is the Royal Umpire Caravan Park at Croston, near Preston. For just about the most comprehensive stock of camping and caravanning equipment you've ever seen, displayed indoors on a site twice the size of two large football pitches, go to Todds Mobile Leisure at Lostock Hall near Preston (for addresses see appendix).

Northumbria

A first sighting of the magnificent Durham Cathedral is an unforgettable experience. I'd driven up the A1(M) and towards the city and there it stood, as though floating on a dream cloud - and I swear I'd only been on the extra strong mints. Keep an eye on the traffic in front though if you're driving. Park on the outskirts of Durham and go 'walk-about'. Along by the River Wear, visit the Castle.

The Grange Caravan Club Site just off the A1(M) with good clean facilities is open all year, non-members are admitted and there's a special field for tents.

'Northumbria' reaches down as far as Saltburn-by-the-Sea and Guisborough and the Cleveland Hills, along the coast to Whitley Bay and Seahouses to Berwick-upon-Tweed. Kielder Forest and Kielder Water come into this area but there's only one campsite in the Forest, half a mile from the Forestry Commission Visitor Centre. This is a site we haven't stayed at but it's open during the main season and accepts tents and trailer tents.

Going inland again Northumbria goes as far as Barnard Castle and Haltwhistle. Other places to visit in this region include the Beamish North of England Open Air Museum, Killhope Lead Mining Centre and Holy Island. The latter is reached by a causeway which can only be crossed at low tide - another exciting experience for me.

Again camping sites are fairly thin on the ground in Northumbria but the Camping and Caravanning Club run two on the coast, one at Beadnell Bay, the other at Dunstan Hill. Both accept non-members and take tents and trailer tents. The Caravan Club has a site at Powburn, Alnwick and one on Newcastle Racecourse, both of which accept tents and non-members.

South East

Historic towns such as Canterbury and Chichester, rolling downs, ancient ports, orchards and oast houses are just some of the magnets in this corner of England. Then there are resorts such as Brighton, Eastbourne, Margate and Worthing. The Seven Sisters Country Park located at Exceat, east of Seaford, is where we spent our first camping weekends, before it was turned into a country park. I believe there's only pitching for backpackers these days. What superb walks and surroundings, with chalk cliffs, shingle beaches and downland.

Most of the coastal towns can boast more than the occasional sightseeing attraction. Some of the latest places to open to the public include The Historic Dockyard at Chatham in Kent - with the added thrill of an hour long cruise on a paddlesteamer. There's a Sealife Centre at Hastings, the Eurotunnel Exhibition Centre at Folkestone and at Dover the 'White Cliffs Experience' which covers from Vera Lynn back to Roman times. There are probably more stately homes, gardens and castles than anywhere else in England. We gave up counting those listed in the English Heritage and National Trust handbooks.

Camping sites are quite regularly spaced with a good concentration in the Chichester and Hastings areas. It's interesting to note that Folkestone, Hythe and Romney Marsh is claimed to be the 'sunniest region on mainland UK'.

Southern England

With the closure of the Thames and Chiltern Tourist Board there have been a couple of changes in the areas covered by tourist boards and the Southern Tourist Board now covers Berkshire, Buckinghamshire and Oxfordshire in addition to Hampshire, parts of Dorset and the Isle of Wight.

What a fantastic area - all right we're southerners and biased. It includes The Isle of Wight, a self-contained holiday destination and one of my favourites; the Chiltern Hills, the famous university city of Oxford, the River Thames and Windsor Castle.

The New Forest has its roving deer and ponies and stacks of hideaways but this is not a region of dark woodland; great stretches of open heathland are all part of the scene. The New Forest is dotted with Forestry Commission sites. Find out in advance just which facilities are offered because they vary from no loos at all to the 'fully equipped' with disabled person's washrooms. Find out too whether you need to book. The New Forest Museum and Visitor Centre at Lyndhurst should perhaps be the first contact.

Moving on down towards the coast we come to Beaulieu with its famous Motor Museum and nearby Bucklers Hard where Nelson's ships were built. Signs of England's maritime heritage can be found all along the Solent especially around Portsmouth. Another interesting place to visit is Eling Tide Mill at Totton near Southampton.

The Dorset Coast Path, a section of the South-west Peninsula Coast Path, runs from Poole to Lyme Regis and comes under the Area of Outstanding Natural Beauty. The Isle of Purbeck has several viewpoints on the road running through the Purbeck Hills and it's easy to see why Lulworth Cove is so popular. A selection of good sites along here, but most are inland.

West Country
There are so many tucked away corners in the West Country that it's difficult to know where to begin. Think of that coastline going from Weymouth in Dorset down to Land's End and back up again through Bude, Ilfracombe, Lynmouth and Weston-super-Mare. All those coves, tiny fishing harbours and beaches.

Picturesque villages are another side of the West Country and great areas of moorland with Bodmin, Dartmoor and Exmoor to stretch your legs. Walkers should set out prepared for all weathers.

There's plenty of historical interest in Wiltshire and if you're in the area you won't want to miss the famous Plymouth Hoe. Moving inland Bristol has its Maritime Heritage Centre and the SS *Great Britain* as well as Harveys Wine Museum.

Yorkshire and Humberside
Rolling moors, bustling market towns and lots of industrial heritage. Two National Parks - the Dales and the Moors - and the Yorkshire Wolds, Herriot and *Last of the Summer Wine* country, you name it, there must be many a space for breathing your own patch of fresh air in this region. Then there's York itself, the spa town of Harrogate and coastal resorts which include Bridlington, Scarborough and Whitby.

We mustn't forget Hull, the National Fishing Heritage Centre at Grimsby and the Humber Bridge. Some good walking country in this region with over 20 long distance and challenge walks in the Wolds area with bird or wildlife reserves at Bempton Cliffs, Hornsea Mere and Spurn Head.

Humberside County Council publishes two useful free booklets. One is *Caravan and Camping Holidays in Humberside* with a list of sites, the other *Walking Holidays in the Wolds* giving details and a sketch map of 39 walks which range from 2 to 12$^{1}/_{2}$ miles.

SCOTLAND AND WALES
These two countries are just packed with 'hidden corners'. The Scottish Borders is an area that many motorists dash through. Stop for a few days in the Jedburgh, Peebles area, visit the Peter Anderson's Woollen Mill at Galashiels and Traquair House near Innerleithen. Stay at the Rosetta or Crossburn Caravan Park.

The relatively new Jedforest Deer and Farm Park at Camptown by Jedburgh is well worth at least half a day. In addition to the animals and a children's corner there are several waymarked walks across the hills. The Jedwater Caravan Park is also recommended.

Mid Wales, with Aberystwyth and Machynlleth somewhere at its centre, is an unspoilt region. The Camping and Caravanning Site at Rhandirmwyn near Llandovery won the AA 'Best Site in Wales' award in 1992. One excellent publication for more detailed information is *A Visitors Guide to Mid Wales*, the Official Guide by Roger Thomas, published by Jarrold Publishing and the Wales Tourist Board.

St Davids, Britain's smallest city and the district along this part of the Welsh coast have much peace and quiet to offer. Activity Holidays too are a feature. We can only advise readers to get out the maps and site guides and discover a few of the 'gems' in Scotland, Wales and Ireland.

CHAPTER NINE

Camping Abroad

Touring the continent for the first time - to the sparkling mountains of Austria and Switzerland, to the sunny beaches of France, Italy or Spain - is an experience that will pack many a photo album. Everything from the ferry crossing or Channel Tunnel is as fresh as a Norwegian morning.

I still get a buzz from collecting my foreign currency from the bank. The shiver that goes along my spine when I see that first mountain of the trip is an even better tonic. Driving on the right has never been a problem, although watch out when leaving a petrol station, particularly if there's no other traffic on the road. Self-service shops and garages make shopping and buying fuel easy enough and there's nearly always someone at a campsite who speaks English. However, good planning makes for the best excursion abroad.

Take time to learn a few words of the language. It not only makes the holiday path smoother but can add to the enjoyment of a trip, especially if going off the beaten track. Buy a phrase book and learn sentences parrot fashion or get down to a study course in the months leading up to your holiday - either taped from a store or at an adult evening centre. Classes can be exciting because you'll be meeting other people who are about to explore that fascinating world out there, and learning a language is something that all the family can take part in. My own feeble attempts at French and German have been extremely useful.

If the premium bonds come up and you decide to start with a long haul trip to places such as North America, Australia or New Zealand, language shouldn't be too much of a problem. Well, apart from little differences. In the USA a camping site is a campground or RV Park - an RV is a Recreational Vehicle or what we call a motorhome. It's also worth noting that some RV establishments do not accept tents. Other differences in America are: their site is our pitch, and the US cot is what we call a camp bed.

PLANNING A HOLIDAY ON THE CONTINENT

So where do you start once the tent, equipment and vehicle is ready for action? (Make sure the car has been properly serviced close to the holiday or your breakdown insurance may not be valid.)

First of all decide on 'where' to go. Young children won't want a never-ending journey. As mentioned in Chapter Five, safe and sandy beaches can be found in Brittany, Normandy, Holland and Belgium. Pop over on one of the reasonably priced short-break tickets to start with, or take the plunge as we did and set off for Switzerland after just two short camping weekends in England! What level of adventure can your family cope with? We suffered no catastrophes and learnt a lot but remember our children were past the toddler stage.

Send for one or two brochures and the perfect location may jump out from its pages. Consider the idea of handing over the booking of the complete holiday to the experts. We'll give a few more suggestions later in this chapter.

Documents and essential items needed for each country vary and even these are changing all the time. Get in touch with your motoring or camping organization for up-to-date information. A first aid kit is mandatory in some countries, as is a spare set of light bulbs. A sturdy warning triangle is a necessity and you may want an International Driving Permit. A spare set of keys and a tow rope could also be useful. Paperwork for the car should include MOT certificate, driving licence and car registration document.

You may want to simply book your own ferry crossing and leave the camping site until arrival at a location. This is what the freedom of camping should be all about. The reality is that during school holidays and at other peak times, sites in main tourist areas - and close to ferry ports - do get snapped up well in advance.

PAPERWORK

We have one quick personal check list for all travels out of the country: TICKETS, PASSPORTS, MONEY and INSURANCE. Make sure your tickets have arrived and are in a handy place when arriving at the ferry terminal.

British Visitor's Passports valid for one year can be obtained from main post offices, the 10 year variety needs to be applied for in advance. At busy times there can be long delays so don't leave things until the last minute.

Your bank should be able to help with foreign currency and traveller's cheques. They may have a stock or you could have to give a few day's notice. It's possible to change money on the ferry but there can be queueing.

Estimate your needs for fuel, food and site fees for two or three days and don't forget that banks do not necessarily keep the same hours and days as those at home.

If you've decided to 'go it alone', insurance, both vehicle and personal, can be taken out at the local brokers - this might be an advantage if you need to claim, but it's advisable to compare the leaflets of several companies. Insurance too is available through motoring organisations, clubs and ready-erected tenting companies. A certain amount of medical expenses and medicines can be reclaimed when an E111 form has been obtained. The E111 is available at post offices. This will give details and countries of use. Just read, fill in and send away, leaving plenty of time before your holiday.

Like the E111, a Green Card is not the answer to all insurance problems but it is still advisable to apply for one and does cover certain aspects. Some insurance companies charge for them, some don't. Make sure your tent and camping gear is covered by one of the insurances. A Camping Carnet too may be needed before a site will accept your outfit or your passport may have to be left at the reception desk.

Maps and a detailed route plan are a necessity. Again, it's possible to DIY but all these extras are usually provided if you take out one of the booking packages available. The independent company 'Routefinder' will provide a tailormade computer route which gives non-motorway roads as well as the 'quickest', 'shortest', 'scenic' way. Charge is around a fiver.

Tourist Boards should be able to help with a list of fuel, food and site prices as well as general information such as Bank Holidays and speed limits. Watch out for 'no drinking and driving' laws; in some cases the upper limit is so low that it would be madness to drive even after a half of light ale.

BOOKING THE EASY WAY

The Camping and Caravanning Club, Eurocamp Independent and Select Site Reservations are three companies offering a booking service to campers taking their own tent and equipment. Everything from ferry and campsite reservations to personal and car breakdown insurance - plus Euro Disney. As a package or separately.

On our recent camping trip to northern Italy when we used our own unit Eurocamp Independent took care of all our bookings. After scanning the brochure and deciding on Lake Maggiorre it was a matter of one phone call to secure and then one single form to fill out. Italian is not one of my

Book the easy way - Eurocamp Independent

languages and as we were all busy at work it was the ideal way to book.

It might be as well to send for one of these 'easy to book' brochures anyway. The crossings available as well as a selection of sites and resorts will be laid out before you. Where do you live and where are you making for? Is the shortest Dover-Calais route best for your family? Perhaps not if Brittany is the chosen region. Some holidaymakers like to relax and spend a night on the ferry, say crossing from Harwich to the Hook of Holland or Plymouth-Santander. For Norway you'll need to go from Newcastle to either Stavanger or Bergen.

French Motorail is an option that can be very useful. France, Italy and Austria are served. You arrive in France, drive up ramps onto the train, find your sleeping compartment and are whisked away through the night. This cuts out a lot of road kilometres, believe me.

SETTING OFF

Read all the documents as soon as they hit the doormat. You'll need to arrive at least 45 minutes before sailing. A map of the ferry port is usually supplied with the tickets but routes to the docks are usually well signposted anyway. Driving up the ramp and onto the ferry is where I get my next 'fix'. You will be directed to a line of vehicles. Secure your handbrake, make sure you've got all you need for the crossing and then enjoy - but keep a clear head. There will be plenty of time for a glass of vino in the sun once the family is settled on site.

WHICH COUNTRY?

What a choice. This can only be a quick round-up. In the main, campsites are similar to those in Britain. By that we mean a whole range of types and sizes. All the advice on choosing a site given in Chapter Six applies.

It's not until you travel the roads of France that the size of the country begins to sink in. We've briefly mentioned the north and south of France but there are so many hidden corners and villages with a municipal site where you can buy groceries from the French version of a corner shop.

One unspoilt area is the Loir Valley. No I haven't forgotten to add an E, this is the baby brother of the feminine Loire. It is slightly closer to the Channel with the famous motor racing centre of Le Mans to its north. There's cycling, canoeing, windsurfing and just about every outdoor activity you can think of. Need I add that the food and wine is to be recommended. Even a stop to buy a sticky bun becomes a memorable occasion.

The Italian Lakes make a good holiday spot because you get mountains, lakes and usually warm weather. Lakeside roads tend to be crowded at peak times so pick a centre carefully. Need we say, Spain is a popular country. Again, search out the less crowded areas.

In Scandinavia early in the season, we found that the smallest site would be spotlessly clean and have all the facilities needed for a comfortable stay. Some of the lakeside spots are so pretty. Take the anti-mossie lotion at certain times of the year and watch out if you camp close to a Norwegian fjord. The sea can be out of sight and miles away but the water is still tidal. Luckily we were sitting outside our VW camper when the water crept silently towards our feet!

Denmark has good sites and sandy beaches and nowhere are you more than 35 miles from the sea. Then there's the famous Legoland and reminders of Hans Christian Andersen. Sweden and Finland are also equipped with some excellent campsites and the attraction in the latter vast countries is the 'great outdoors'. Miles of unspoilt countryside and thousands of lakes. There are also tourist and historical centres. I particularly remember Helsinki for its hot weather and pavement restaurants, so unexpected and just like the Mediterranean on our visit.

'Holland in springtime' is one of my favourites, then there's Austria and Switzerland with superb mountain scenery. Belgium has many historical attractions as well as the forest of the Ardennes.

The 'ice and fire' of Iceland take some beating; for a family this would be a really adventurous trip. Roads outside the main centres cannot be relied on if there's been a severe winter. In any case a vehicle with four wheel drive and good ground clearance is needed so it's as well to hire a car and camping equipment from an Icelandic rental firm.

America, where do we start? Sleeping a night in an Indian teepee at Yakima in the State of Washington was a great experience. True we were touring in a large RV on this occasion and most people have their own dreams for visiting a particular area of the USA. Families with young and not so young children will probably make for Disneyland or Disneyworld.

It is possible to hire a car and tent with equipment and friends of ours took their own tiny 3 berth lightweight, a few pieces of equipment and just hired a car.

The State of Washington has lots of unspoilt areas to attract lovers of the great outdoors. Activities include horseback riding, cycling and walking as well as lots of watersports. Starting near Seattle there's a circular motoring route called the Cascade Loop which takes in the North Cascade Mountains, Winthrop frontier village and Lake Chelan with float plane excursions. The Yakima area makes an interesting detour with miles of vineyards and an Indian Cultural Centre. A taste of 'Twin Peaks' and 'old America' in about four or five hundred miles.

One way to enjoy the great outdoors in America without having to worry about taking a tent is to rent a Kampgrounds of America cabin. These are one and two room log cabins located on the famous KOA sites. An easier way of camping, and campground facilities are used. KOA also sell and will have waiting for you at your first KOA site a complete camping pack. This will include a 2 or 4 person tent plus Coleman stove, lantern and cooler, enamel pot and pan set as well as items such as a dish cloth and towel.

And to end this 'world round-up', in Canada it is possible to rent a vehicle and either hire or buy camping equipment through a firm called Canada Campers Inc. In New Zealand a similar service can be arranged with MAUI through the New Zealand Travel Information Service in London. In Australia Koala Camper Rentals offer a 4 X 4 Toyota Station Wagon fitted with a Quick Erect Rooftop Camper conversion with all equipment necessary for camping in the outback.

What am I doing sitting at a keyboard - let's get out there!

CHAPTER TEN
Ready-erected Tenting Holidays

Camping at its most Civilised' is how Canvas Holidays describes their own particular brand of ready-erected tenting holidays. And they should know. After 28 years in the business they are still improving their outfits with the latest additions being a personal toilet, wash-basin and shower cabin next to your tent (at selected locations).

Old hands at the camping game may think all these luxuries are a bit over the top but holidays are to be enjoyed. As an outdoor addict the author can think of nothing more pleasurable than waking up under canvas having gone to bed freshly scrubbed and scented - having used our own private shower room.

But there's no need to go to these extremes, any kind of luxury is often more expensive. Canvas Holidays, Eurocamp and other firms offer many up-to-the-minute facilities and the sites themselves are already well equipped, lots with laundry rooms and take-away meals. It should be noted that if we mention a facility it is not necessarily unique to one particular company. This book can only be a guide to the kind of luxuries to be expected.

Prices and facilities provided vary so much that you need to sit down and compare brochures before a decision is made. For instance the cost may be given for a 12 day holiday, it may be 14. As always, we tend to 'get what we pay for'. We've seen ready-erected tents positioned on handkerchief sized pitches, half the size of those used by other companies. The tents themselves too may be of different qualities.

Another of the great things about ready-erected tent holidays is that everything can be booked at one go. The tent, the crossing - most operators and routes are available - health and vehicle insurance, Motorail and overnight accommodation which in some cases can be tent, mobile home or hotel. Stopping a night or two en-route gives a welcome and necessary break if you're travelling long distances, much depending on the final destination (see Chapter Nine for suggestions).

In addition to tickets and notes on the ferry crossing, the Travel Pack issued by good firms will include a detailed route and a map which will be from Michelin or another equally reliable source as well as a traveller's guide to the route and holiday area; individual directions and notes on the campsite/s; a children's pack; British Telecom, DHSS and Consular advice and a GB sticker.

These 'camping without tears' type holidays can be found in France, Belgium, Luxembourg, Germany, Austria, Switzerland, Italy, Spain, Corsica and Sardinia as well as England, Ireland and Denmark and Sweden.

All kinds of 'special offers' are available, in some cases up to four children can be accommodated free. Under 4s might be taken without cost and even under 14s in the low season. Single parents and teenagers attract certain reductions and if you take a holiday late or early in the season the savings can be quite substantial.

Eurocamp has special off-peak holidays for couples and if your children have flown the nest look for those offered to 'La Troisieme Age'. One or both partners need to be 55 years or over to take advantage of these 'third age' breaks. Out of the main season is a good time for a holiday. Roads and campsites are uncrowded and usually quieter after the children have gone back to their desks.

TENTS AND EQUIPMENT PROVIDED

The size and lay-out of tents vary. If you want a space between the bedrooms then study the floor plan given in the brochure. You may find a corner kitchen separating the inner compartments - the set-up we favour, especially when taking children because the cooker is out of the living area. In other tents the bedrooms may be situated along the back wall. Pre-erected tents usually sleep six people with a double bed in one sleeping compartment and in the other, two rooms divided by a curtain. These might have single, bunk beds or cots.

You will not be sleeping in old-fashioned wooden camp beds with only a length of canvas for comfort but strong framed bedsteads with quite deep mattresses. Talk about camping in luxury.

The kitchen will contain a double burner cooker (could be four burners and a grill, another point to check if anyone is a keen cook) and usually situated on a multi-shelved unit. Crockery and cutlery for six is part of the usual inventory along with cooking utensils and a whole range of extras such as cheese grater and a salad bowl. The dining furniture is of the sturdy garden patio variety and for even more home comforts there will be one or two electric lights and a full size fridge. The floor will be covered by a heavy duty groundsheet.

Outside the tent there may be a couple of hammocks or sun loungers and sometimes if the site management allow them, a barbecue. In the main all you need to take is bedding, towels and tea cloths and of course some food to start the holiday - all right, and the 'thousand and two' bits and pieces needed for a family excursion!

Baby packs with a high chair, play pen, travel cot and bath are also available - imagine taking that lot in the family saloon.

CAMPING SITES USED

Again, study the brochure details. A chosen site may have four stars but do you need all those extra activities? They can cause the noise and disturbances that you are trying to get away from. The best companies will tell you whether a site is 'laid back' or 'lively'. In most cases there will be a swimming pool. The exceptions will be if there is a beach or lake close by and perhaps if the site is deep into the mountains where peace and quiet is the great attraction. Many will have a shop and/or takeaway and restaurant. There may be tennis courts, bicycles for hire, mini-golf and horse-riding.

Some firms concentrate on watersports at appropriate points with kyaks and windsurfing boards included in the cost. The services of a special courier might be part of the package or it could be an extra.

However, on arrival at the camping site all information needed will be found at the company 'office', usually a large frame tent. If the noticeboard does not contain an answer to your query ask a rep or courier. To be really clued up read every piece of literature before leaving home. The fine detail may not be remembered but you will at least know where to find a relevant paragraph if required.

It's also a good idea to take along the brochure. If any aspect of the holiday is not up to standard discuss this at the time with a courier. A complaint may be quickly and easily put right. If you've got the brochure it's easier to prove what was actually promised.

SPECIAL INTERESTS FOR CHILDREN

Not only will your fully equipped tent be sited at an inspected establishment, the brochure itself will give you a good idea of how stylish or otherwise the gear and location is going to be. Choose carefully. Toddlers do not need the same type of holiday as teenagers.

Most firms have Children's Couriers who will organize events for the youngsters and there may be a baby-sitting service but possibly not in residence at all locations.

Another good idea for keeping children happy are the comprehensive Children's Packs issued by Canvas Holidays and Eurocamp. These are a range of leaflets and booklets packed with quizzes, 'items to spot' and so on which will get the kids interested in the whole travel and outdoor life scene. Like the little *I Spy* books, invaluable, especially once children have moved on past the bucket and sandcastle stage.

Never fear though, there will be something for all age groups at most locations. Several companies have introduced small junior or beginner's tents for older children. These are meant as an extra, independent bedroom which kids just love.

Canvas Holidays and Eurocamp have a Wildlife Guide at some of their camps. Most of the walks and excursions will be suitable for children because the leaders may have their own family along. I was going to add 'depending on age' but with papoose baby carriers, very few groups are left out these days so even that statement would not be correct.

We've used the CH Luz St Sauveur site in the French Pyrenees and L'Orangerie in Brittany, both to be recommended. Walks or half day trips organised by the Wildlife Guide are announced on the noticeboard and you can join in or give them a miss - the swimming pool may be a stronger attraction on that particular day.

At Luz St Sauveur our Guide, a member of the Royal Society for the Protection of Birds, took us on some wonderful rambles and not only pointed out griffin vultures soaring along the mountain tops but gave us the opportunity to take pictures of orchids and other flowers. The latter were nestling between rocks or hidden in meadows where a newcomer to mountain species would never have found them.

On these excursions we took our own cars and at one of the bays in Brittany we were able to get quite close to a friendly dolphin. Rambles also started from the site. One I remember ending up with a demonstration of owl pellet dissection, a process that was fascinating as well as educational for young and not so young!

Gone are the days of tinned beans and cold showers every morning. Modern camping does not go hand in hand with discomfort. Mind you, there's nothing to stop anyone who stays in a ready-erected tent from opening the odd tin of spaghetti and taking a cooling shower on a hot day. Freedom of choice and flexibility is what any type of camping is all about.

The great thing about pre-sited tents is that there's no tent to erect at the end of a day's drive, no gear to stack into the car or trailer and you'll be sleeping off the floor on a proper bed. Many families have become hooked on ready-erected tent holidays and return to one company time after time, just changing the country or region. Others realise how much they love the outdoor life and go on to buy their own equipment which will bring the cost down in future years.

On the other hand you may get no further than the mobile home section of the brochure. But that's not 'real camping', or is it?

YAKIMA, WASHINGTON STATE, USA

In the American State of Washington and possibly in other areas it's possible to rent an Indian teepee. We can only speak about those at the RV Resort Park, Yakima, which were great fun but only basic canvas teepees with a concrete floor and no equipment. Air beds and cots (camp beds) can be rented and there's an undercover picnic area as well as toilet block, pool and hot tub. This is a modern RV Park and motorhomes are well catered for with hardstandings and full hook-ups.

Teepees to rent at Yakima

CHAPTER ELEVEN
Joining a Club or Association

Whether you join a club or not is a very personal choice. I sometimes think that people who say they are not interested do not know what they are missing. All right, a rally field with around 3,000 units is not everyone's cup of Earl Grey but that is not what a Club is all about. Confession time. I had been a Member of the Camping and Caravanning Club for 20 years before attending a large rally. We joined because we wanted to keep in touch with what was happening on the camping scene. Hear about new tents and equipment, obtain a Camping Carnet for our trips abroad and to take advantage of the range of services that were being introduced.

I am now in my 25th year and can't imagine being without comfortable Club Sites and the monthly magazine to keep me posted. If camping in smaller numbers appeals to your family there are District Associations within the Club, small 'minimum facility' sites and Special Interest Sections.

Readers may be wondering why we are giving so many lines to one camping club. The answer is easy. There is only one main club in Great Britain and Ireland catering for family tent campers and that is The Camping and Caravanning Club, now based in Coventry.

There's the Backpackers Club which as its name suggests is aimed at backpacking, the Companions Camping Group for solo campers who can take along any type of unit and there is The Association of Lightweight Campers which is a Section of The Camping and Caravanning Club - more of this later.

The Camping and Caravanning Club started in a field at Wantage near Oxford with just six members. The year was 1901 and it was with the Association of Cycle Campers. Truly a group of tenting and cycle enthusiasts. The way that the Club has been so enthusiastically organised and has forged ahead can only prove what lively and adventurous people campers are. In 1909 Captain Robert Falcon Scott RN (Scott of the Antarctic) became President of the Club. In 1913 the first Club Tour abroad was organised to Holland.

King George VI became Patron of the Club followed by The Duke of Edinburgh who each year sends greetings to the Club's AGM and officially opened the new Club Site at Sandringham.

There have been name changes to the Club along the way, the best known being The Camping Club of Great Britain and Ireland which took in the years from 1919 to 1983. As many members were beginning to change from tents to caravans and motor caravans it was finally decided to use the name The Camping and Caravanning Club.

This did not go un-noticed and there were cries that caravanning is not 'real camping'. To my mind 'camping' is for everyone who derives pleasure from living in the great outdoors in a 'portable shelter' of a socially acceptable type. They might revel in peace and solitude or enjoy the friendship of other people they meet along the way. Does the title matter?

The Camping and Caravanning Club now owns or manages around 80 Sites, one of the latest additions being on the Isle of Wight. From a field in Wantage to an all 'mod cons' site at Sandringham has only happened with lots of hard work by many volunteers who give up their weekends and holidays. Their slogan 'The Friendly Club' says it all.

So what does a subscription to The Camping and Caravanning Club buy?

Free with Membership are two Site Guides. One, *Your Place in the Country*, is a colour publication giving a page to each of the Club Sites. Prices and facilities are included, a 'how to get there' sketch map, a photograph or two and a write-up on what to see and do in the area.

The other, *Your Big Sites Book*, is a comprehensive list of over 5,000 sites, large and small in Britain and Ireland. A free Ordnance Survey Map accompanies this publication.

In addition a monthly colour magazine will drop through your letterbox and with this is an 'Out and About' Supplement listing what the District Associations and Special Interest Sections will be doing - and where.

As the Club expanded from 6 to well over 100,000 members, District Association Meets and the Sections have become larger and more active. Relaxing these days does not necessarily mean sitting outside the tent in the sun. Increasing numbers of campers are joining the Club Sections. The Association of Lightweight Campers being among them - which was really where it all started when bicycles were the means of transport. Today this Section still caters for cyclists but the main interest is in lightweight tent camping. How you arrive at a site is irrelevant.

Families too are welcome at other Section meets which include: 'Mountain Activity', 'Boating', 'Photographic', 'Trailer Tent' 'Canoe-Camping' and

'Folk Dance and Song'.

Other Club Services include 'Foreign Touring' - pitch reservation, ferry crossing and travel insurance - and RAC Membership at reduced rates. There's a Club Direct Loan Scheme and Club Care for all kinds of insurance.

Address for further information: The Camping and Caravanning Club, Greenfields House, Westwood Way, Coventry CV4 8JH. (01203) 694995 Fax (01203) 694886.

CONSERVATION AND PROTECTION SOCIETIES

Most people have a favourite charity which may or may not have anything to do with conservation. However, once the outdoor life begins to grip it is difficult not to become involved. A complete list of associations would use up a good many trees so we will give only a few suggestions. The Club already mentioned has a conservation group organising working parties and several of the following associations have their local and children's sections.

English Heritage

Membership Department, PO Box 1BB, London W1A 1BB. (0171) 973 3400. Established by an Act of Parliament in 1984 the primary task of English Heritage is to care for England's inheritance of a great number of historic buildings and ancient monuments.

The annual subscription buys free admission to all English Heritage properties; free or reduced admission to special events and concerts held at the properties. Reduced admission to over 100 sites in Scotland, Wales, the Isle of Man and the Jorvik Viking Centre in York. Members Pack with handbook, map, events diary, car sticker and badges. Quarterly magazine.

The National Trust

Membership Enquiries, PO Box 39, Bromley, Kent BR1 1NH. (0181) 464 1111. As well as being concerned with country houses and their contents the National Trust also preserves gardens, landscaped parks and countryside locations such as woods, lakes, mountains and coastline plus prehistoric and Roman sites, farms and even villages and hamlets.

Yearly subscription entitles Members to: free admission to most National Trust properties, handbook, three magazines, two regional newsletters and mail order catalogue.

The Ramblers' Association

1/5 Wandsworth Road, London SW8 2XX.

Formed over 50 years ago The Ramblers' Association plays a leading role in campaigns to protect and open up the countryside. Waymarking, protection of footpaths and public access to once forbidden areas - you name it.

Subscription not only helps with this important work but entitles Members to *Rambling Today*, a bi-monthly magazine, yearbook, discount at a number of outdoor equipment shops, programme of walks with a local group. Social events are arranged.

The Wildlife Trusts

The Green, Witham Park, Waterside South, Lincoln LN5 7JR. (01522) 544400 Fax (01522) 511616.

The Wildlife Trusts work differently being split into county groups from the beginning. Details of county contacts from the above address. The Wildlife Trusts collectively look after around 2,000 nature reserves.

Membership brings: free entrance to Trust Reserves, handbook, magazine, local newsletters, walks and 'visits' as well as helping to purchase conservation sites.

The Royal Society for the Protection of Birds

The Lodge, Sandy, Bedfordshire SG19 2BR. (01767) 680551.

In 1889 Mrs Robert Williamson, wife of a Manchester solicitor, held a meeting for people who shared her horror of the destruction of birds to obtain their feathers for adorning hats. This was the beginning of the RSPB. The rest, as they say, is history. Membership advantages: free admission to most RSPB reserves; regional activities, talks and mail order gifts; Young Ornithologists' Club.

CHAPTER TWELVE
Walking, Special Interest and Activity Holidays

There comes a time when just setting up tent and equipment may not satisfy the adventurous side of the family's nature. We see other campers lacing up their walking boots, un-hitching their boats, inflating a dinghy, taking the kyak from the car roof, mountain bikes from their rack and so on.

Before you start any of these activities for the first time get expert advice and/or tuition. The safety of the family must be number one priority. We hear when things go wrong at one of the commercial activity centres but things can go just as wild if the family acts in an irresponsible way. An ability to swim a certain distance is usually necessary for watersports and selected activities have a lower age limit.

The author doesn't like to keep giving warnings and in the outdoor life we have to accept that there are some dangers but where our children are concerned we should give thought to what could happen, take all the precautions possible - and then join in the planning and go for it!

For notes on the Special Interest Sections of The Camping and Caravanning Club see Chapter Eleven. If you've decided on a particular activity do your research, if not, what about going on a multi-activity break to get an idea of the options? Then contact the Tourist Boards for details of courses in their area. Ask also for a list of 'safe centres'. Accrediting activity centres seems to be a bit hit and miss at present but Charles Letts publishes *UK Activity Holiday* in association with the Tourist Boards.

The Wales Tourist Board issue *Wales - Britain's Activity Country* which not only gives addresses of establishments but lists Governing Bodies from the British Canoe Union to the YCA (Yacht Charter Association) which means you can send away for more information.

Check the accommodation arrangements. There are stacks of day, half-day and even half-hour activities and a few longer courses for non-residents. One company that offers 'freelance' family holidays is PGL Adventure (known for their children's - or Parents Get Lost - unaccompanied holidays). Campers and caravanners can stay at a nearby site and join in the day's activities.

In some cases an evening meal is part of the deal on PGL Holidays, which makes things easier if the cook has been windsurfing or whatever all day. Some activities are only available 'with accommodation'. This can be anything from bunks to four poster beds, and DIY washing-up to six course dinners.

Less hectic Special Interests such as birdwatching, painting and walking are also available. Some of these such as those run by Ramblers and HF Holidays are using residential centres. High Trek Snowdonia is a friendly family-run business with different grade walks and a range of accommodation which can include a night spent in a mountain tent. I achieved one ambition with High Trek Snowdonia and walked the 'not so easy' route to the top of Snowdon. Fantastic - and it's only in the last five years, as the bus pass loomed, that I took up walking in a more serious way.

If like me you've never truly mastered an Ordnance Survey map and compass start with one of the many Guided Walks run by local authorities and National Parks. They may be free of charge or cost very little. Contact the tourist board of your chosen holiday area and/or if you're near a National Park look out for their free news-sheet with a Diary of Walks. These could be purely rambles or with a historical or other interest.

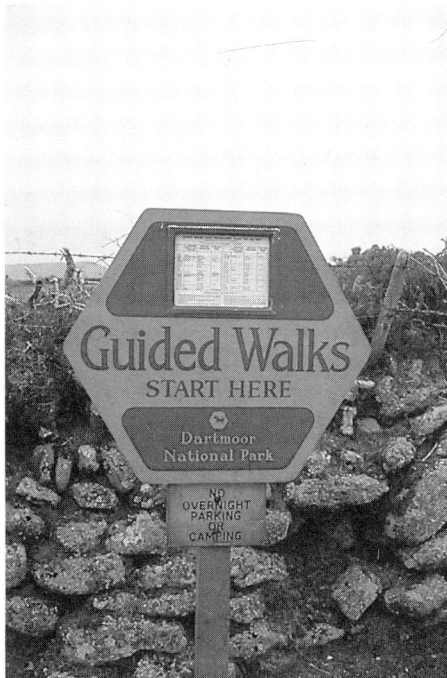

Take advantage of guided walks organised by local authorities and National Parks

CHAPTER THIRTEEN:

Outdoor Gear

The type of gear we choose has to be suitable for the level of camping or walking to be tackled. Icy mountain tops are not the usual venue for family campers and if they are, the participants should be well experienced and know that specialist clothing is necessary. This chapter is about outdoor

Clothing should be suitable for the level of activity

wear for campers and ramblers and generally available from camping centres and shops - who may well stock specialist gear as well.

The author is speaking from a personal point of view and a tall woman's at that. Manufacturer's claims can be useful but there's nothing like experience, hence the different manufacturer's names that will crop up in the following paragraphs. You may decide that an anorak is an anorak and for car-camping anything more 'specialist' is not required, especially if you use an umbrella on site.

Walking or rambling is slightly different. Consider where you will be walking. Most of my rambling is 'low level' either in Bedfordshire or East Anglia. Go for short walks and try out any existing gear. Don't lay out too much cash until you get an idea of the type of garments needed. Don't set off for the hills without being suitably clad and equipped with emergency items. It's not until you've seen mist rolling across your path like a pop concert gone wild that you realise just how easy it is to get completely lost.

JACKETS

Let's start with another don't - don't 'impulse buy'. It's wise to ask the sales assistants for their guidance; if they've had a number of so-called waterproof jackets returned by customers they won't be recommending those. Don't go for any high pitch sales talk though. Is a £250 jacket necessary if you're going for a week's camping holiday on the south coast? True, it may well be suitable but could be a bit over the top - unless you fall in love with a particular jacket/are rich/our summers really do get worse.

Having said that my Karrimor Baltoro Gore-Tex jacket was high in the range and worth the price. It is light in weight, breathable and waterproof as well as being good to look at. I've walked for hour after hour, all day in fact, in lashing rain and only suffered a few damp spots at the front because I hadn't fastened the neck properly. The Baltoro is described as being a 'high specification hill and fell walking jacket'.

At the time of writing the Karrimor Hoolie jacket in Polartec Windbloc is being tested. This is a fleece garment designed to be totally windproof and with 'enhanced water repellency'. The secret is a very thin breathable layer of material between inner and outer fabric.

Yet again, we usually get what we pay for and it's not worth spending out hundreds of pounds on gear for growing children. The expensive garments will probably be well finished, stylishly cut, last longer and in many cases be produced in the latest colour schemes. However, there are several economy priced clothing manufacturers or importers. Risol, with their Regatta range, is one of them. Regatta garments can be seen all over hill and dale and we've found them to be good value for money but do try the clothing on because in some cases a size larger than usual is necessary. This also goes for other manufacturers.

All clothing must be comfortable to wear. This statement may sound obvious but in the excitement it's easy to get carried away. Make allowances for thermal underwear or jerseys that may be worn. The layering system is recommended. Underwear, be it thermal or otherwise; shirt; fleece garment or jersey and then top jacket.

The latter can be a single garment of breathable waterproof fabric or you may decide to go for a showerproof fleece or polycotton jacket plus a lightweight fully waterproof top coat to keep out the rain and wind. Also leave room for that important layer of air. The billowy Michelin man type rally coats and the ubiquitous wax jackets may be good for on-site wear but with more serious walking you will quickly warm up and cool down and it's so much easier to take off a layer than to have a thick heavy coat to carry.

Try on the jacket and walk about in it. Too heavy and you'll get hot and tired quickly, too tight and you may get cold. My Mountain Equipment blouson coat in soft and cosy microfibre material is great when putting up a tent. For walking I like a longer jacket that covers my backside. Another point to be watched is how much the jacket is likely to ride up when carrying a rucksack. Get the length right and the neck sitting easily.

For years my favourite camping anorak was made from a lightly proofed no-rustle polycotton. For walking I also carried high-rustle waterproof trousers and jacket and was always dubious about the latest waterproof, breathable materials - until the Karrimor Baltoro which is a new addition to my wardrobe. Craghoppers is a firm that has been on the outdoor scene for a good many years and is updating its outdoor garments all the time. Look for an overflap to keep water from oozing through the zip, pockets that are useable and a well fitting hood.

As a regular walker I am always hearing about jackets that become wet inside. Some garments do leak, it's true, but very often the moisture is perspiration or condensation. We all perspire at different levels and even the outside temperature makes a difference to the amount of condensation that breathable fabrics can deal with.

TROUSERS

Most campers will be completely at home in jeans. For country walking they are not a good idea because they become heavy when wet and take ages to dry.

Women's fittings are easier to find these days although the author, having long legs and wide hips, has only found one type of outdoor trousers to suit and those are in a men's size with a large waist, the ever popular Rohan Bags. These have lots of useful pockets, are of a polycotton mixture and can be washed and dried overnight. Worth every penny.

Rohan Bags are not waterproof but if they get wet and the rain stops you can actually see patches drying off as you walk. Whether you buy mens or ladies, make sure the seat is deep enough with the waist at a comfortable level - and that there is actually room to use most of the pockets. Believe it or not some manufacturers still make pockets like mouse traps! This is where Rohan score points again. They provide a pop fastener and small gusset on each of the front pockets which gives extra space.

Rohan also makes Winter Bags but I make do with the summer version adding thermal long johns in cold weather - again your choice will depend on how much out of season walking you are contemplating and where you will be rambling or camping.

Regatta makes some very similar multi-pocketed trousers at a very reasonable price.

WATERPROOFS

To give you an idea of the wide choice to be found, there are 46 companies under the 'waterproofs' heading in the latest COLA catalogue.

Most walkers carry a wet weather set consisting of waterproof trousers and jacket with hood. My waterproof trousers spend most of the time collecting crumbs at the bottom of my rucksack because I don't like putting them on for just a rainshower. If we start out in pouring rain then waterproofs are essential.

Peter Storm and Regatta both make 'value for money' waterproof sets. Make sure they are large enough to cover all the other gear. Waterproof trousers with a zip at the ankle are probably the easiest to put on over walking boots but they will be more expensive. An ankle gusset with pop fasteners is a cheaper way of getting round the problem. A large elasticated waist is also a good idea - and look for taped seams which should stop rain seeping through the stitching holes.

Remember that waterproofs can spend a lot of time rolled up in your rucksack and there may be leaks at the folds or where rubbing of the fabric has occurred.

Karrimor 'Glacier'
35 litre daysack

RUCKSACKS

Walkers also need a rucksack. You'll need somewhere to put those layers as they are taken off and something in which to carry your waterproofs, as well as that extra sweater, lunch and drink etc. You may get children interested in walking if a colourful rucksack is part of the bargain. There are some very reasonably priced models on the market.

Because of the amount of stitching on a rucksack they are not guaranteed waterproof. A seam spray could be used and rucksack liners can be bought although I make do with a strong plastic carrier bag - with no little perforations or you're back to square one. Needless to say, don't leave young children with any plastic bags.

Rucksack size. The name of the model will be a clue. Daysack etc. I find the Karrimor Trail 25 (25 litre capacity) about right for day walking with a 35 litre size for taking on aeroplanes. The latter can be taken into the cabin and will hold enough gear for several days. If I'm also taking a suitcase (for instance on a longer walking holiday abroad) the smaller daysack is large enough.

If I'm in a 'dressy' mood, it's flight bag, suitcase and a very thin nylon rucksack that can be tucked into a pocket or any tiny corner. This little green wonder came as a free gift with an AA book but that's another story. They can be found on the pages of outdoor catalogues. It's interesting to see that Karrimor make rucksacks in a ladies fitting. These have a shorter back length and specially tailored harness and hipbelt to match the female form.

WALKING BOOTS - OR SHOES

Again ask the advice of the sales experts. But before looking at boots decide on socks. To wear with leather I prefer a thin pair made of looped cotton plus a pair of the thick woollen variety. Makers of outdoor gear will say that today's boots are lined and there are special socks that do away with this 'doubling up' but to my mind they act like a comfy cushion. A larger boot size may be necessary but it's worth it, although be careful, too large and you'll trip over. With my Merrell Solo shoes I wear one pair of mediumweight looped cotton socks.

If fitted with care the attractive looking lightweight boots with uppers in a leather/Cordura nylon mixture can be comfortable from day one. No walking-in is needed. But they are not really designed for winter walking in Britain or any other wet and muddy countryside. However, Gore-Tex and Sympatex waterproof linings, socks and sprays are available if you decide to stick to lightweights.

Wellington boots may be good for on-site wear but they have several disadvantages for rambling. They can be cold in use, cause blisters and the soles may be smooth and therefore slippery on mud. Good old-fashioned leather is probably a better choice for damp and cold weather, although even leather may not keep out the wet. My Merrell Cumbrian WTC (weather tight construction) walking boots are leather, they look good and were comfortable straight from the box. Merrell boots can be found at many outdoor centres but the Cumbrians are exclusive to Milletts. A special Merrell footbed is designed to the foot shape and women's fittings are offered.

A coating of special boot wax helps to keep out the water but it needs to be re-applied if you do much walking through wet grass. Follow the instructions on the tin. Some manufacturers advise a thin layer. The dubbin that was once widely used is inclined to soften leather which could be good if you need to ease a spot or two but wax is probably better for waterproofing.

Over the years I have tried different types of boots and shoes: low boots and boots with a higher ankle cuff, leather shoes in the old style and walking shoes that look like trainers but are durable and strengthened (Merrell Solo). The British company High Country used to make a low grey coloured boot that was both leather and lightweight which took me many hundreds of miles with never a blister. Their latest ladies models are known as the Little Blue and Little Green boots.

Karrimor makes a good range of all types of walking boot - in men's and women's fittings. In fact their KSBs were the first ever fabric lightweights. The KSBs come with quite high ankle cuffs for good support. As with any other boot make sure it doesn't grab your ankle like a vice. This is where a women's fitting differs from a man's.

A one piece leather boot, with few seams for water to seep through, may be best from the waterproof aspect but they could need more breaking-in. These variations and choices make trying on and walking around in the footwear an essential exercise.

The general rule is that with the laces undone you should be able to push your foot to the front and get a forefinger between heel and boot. Most people's feet swell during a walk - you will know to what extent this is likely to happen, if at all. Walking downhill in boots that are too short is agony. Get the right fit and you'll be springing along with the lambs.

CHAPTER FOURTEEN
Re-proofing a tent

You may never have to re-proof the family tent. Cotton canvas can last for years with perhaps the odd seam or panel needing a touch of spray. As a camping writer there are certain chores that have to be attempted and reproofing a 20 year old frame tent that looked big enough to accommodate several performing elephants and a group of jugglers sounded daunting - but it was possible!

In fact the tent was a mere 15ft x 18ft and with two of us starting well after mid-morning it was dry enough by 3 o'clock to be taken away to a local hall to complete the drying process. (I hope the naval cadets appreciated our efforts Tina.)

We chose the 'painting' method but if the tent is small and lightweight and you have a large enough container there are products for total immersion of the tent - or jacket, or socks etc. Some types of material can even be reproofed in the washing machine.

We chose Grangers Fabsil for our La Prairie frame tent, went to a local DIY store, bought two paint kettles and two 3in paintbrushes and got stuck in - but not before erecting the tent and preparing the canvas.

The product comes with full instructions which must be carefully studied and as with other 'paint jobs' good preparation is important.

Make any necessary repairs and treat any mildew but whatever you do don't clean grease or dirt off with detergent or washing-up liquid. White Spirit is a possibility. We sponged bird lime off with warm water. Remember too to cover the ground while decanting the Fabsil as it can harm grass. Fabsil is a watery fluid that can be applied directly to the canvas and to prevent 'tide marks' we are urged to keep a wet edge all the time.

To reach the ridge we erected the tent to its half-height or kneeling position and folded the walls and roof to the centre, gradually unfolding as we went along. The canvas should be kept as taut as possible and the size of the tent and the length of your arm will decide when the tent can be fully erected and pegged. Then its just a matter of painting away and down the walls. Using one of those backpack sprays with a long applicator could make things easier. Either way don't choose a windy day.

Pick a fairly still morning but not hot or the fluid will dry too quickly. A chilly January day with a slight breeze is not ideal but it was possible and we 'paintbrush wielders' suffered, not the tent.

The amount of Fabsil required will vary. Older, porous tents will soak up more fluid than one that was treated a year or two ago. A general guide is 18sq metres/litre for nylon, 14sq metres/litre for lightweight canvas and 5sq metres/litre for mediumweight canvas.

A pump spray or ozone friendly aerosol could be used for the occasional panel or seams but these work out expensive for a complete frame tent. Grangers Fabsil bonds well to a range of fabrics such as nylon, polycotton and various mixtures. If in any doubt about which proofer to use check with your retailer or contact Grangers' Technical Department at Grangers International Ltd, Grange Close, Clover Nook Industrial Park, Alfreton, Derbyshire DE55 4QT. (01773) 521521.

This size should cover a scout camp!

APPENDIX

Regional Tourist Boards will often provide free information on 'what to see and do' in their area. If it's a general view of the country that interests you, look for the annual booklets published by the English, Scottish, Northern Ireland and Wales Tourist Boards. The Isle of Man and the Isle of Wight have separate offices.

A list of over 800 Tourist Information Centres in Britain is also published. If you've actually arrived on holiday search out the local Tourist Information Centre (TIC) which in some villages may be found at the local library.

NATIONAL AND REGIONAL TOURIST BOARDS

The English Tourist Board, Thames Tower, Black's Road, Hammersmith, London W6 9EL. (0181) 846 9000

Northern Ireland Tourist Board, St Anne's Court, 59 North Street, Belfast BT1 1NB. (01232) 246609

The Scottish Tourist Board, 23 Ravelston Terrace, Edinburgh EH4 3EU. (0131) 332 2433

The Wales Tourist Board, Brunel House, 2 Fitzalan Road, Cardiff CF2 1UY. (01222) 499909

Isle of Man Tourism, Sea Terminal, Douglas, Isle of Man. (01624) 686760

Isle of Wight Tourist Office, Quay House, Town Quay, Newport, Isle of Wight PO30 2EF. (01983) 524343

Cumbria Tourist Board, (covering the county of Cumbria), Ashleigh, Holly Road, Windermere, Cumbria LA23 2AQ. (015394) 44444

East Anglia Tourist Board (Cambridgeshire, Essex, Hertfordshire, Bedfordshire, Norfolk, Suffolk), Toppesfield Hall, Hadleigh, Suffolk IP7 5DN. (01473) 822922

East Midlands Tourist Board (Derbyshire, Leicestershire, Lincolnshire, Northamptonshire, Nottinghamshire), Exchequergate, Lincoln, Lincolnshire LN2 1PZ. (01522) 531521/3

Heart of England Tourist Board (Gloucestershire, Hereford & Worcester, Shropshire, Staffordshire, Warwickshire, West Midlands), Woodside, Larkhill Road, Worcester, Worcestershire WR5 2EF. (01905) 763436

London Tourist Board (Greater London), 26 Grosvenor Gardens, London SW1W ODU.
To obtain 'Visitorcall' telephone card guide call (0171) 971 0026

North West Tourist Board (Cheshire, Greater Manchester, Lancashire, Merseyside, High Peak District of Derbyshire), Swan House, Swan Meadow Road, Wigan Pier, Wigan, Lancashire WN3 5BB. (01942) 821222

Northumbria Tourist Board (Cleveland, Durham, Northumberland, Tyne and Wear), Aykley Heads, Durham DH1 5UX. (0191) 384 6905

South East England Tourist Board (East and West Sussex, Kent, Surrey), The Old Brew House, Warwick Park, Tunbridge Wells, Kent TN2 5TU. (01892) 540766

Southern Tourist Board (Eastern and Northern Dorset, Hampshire, Oxfordshire, Berkshire, Buckinghamshire, Isle of Wight), 40 Chamberlayne Road, Eastleigh, Hampshire SO5 5JH. (01703) 620006

West Country Tourist Board (Avon, Cornwall, Devon, Dorset (parts of) Somerset, Wiltshire, Isles of Scilly), 60 St David's Hill, Exeter, Devon EX4 4SY. (01392) 76351

Yorkshire & Humberside Tourist Board (Humberside, North Yorkshire, South Yorkshire, West Yorkshire), 312 Tadcaster Road, York YO2 2HF. (01904) 707961

OVERSEAS TOURIST BOARDS

If sending for information be specific. Most issue a general information brochure on their country as well as a list of camping sites and leaflets on various regions.

Austrian National Tourist Office, 30 St George Street, London WIR OAL. (0171) 629 0461

Belgian Tourist Office, 29 Princess Street, London W1R 7TG. (0171) 629 0230

Canada House, 1 Cockspur Street, Trafalgar Square, London SW1Y 5BT. (0171) 679 9492

Danish Tourist Board, 55 Sloane Street, London SW1X 9SR. (0171) 259 5958

French Government Tourist Office, 178 Picadilly, London W1V OAL. (0891) 244123

German National Tourist Office, 65 Curzon Street, London W1Y 7PE. (0171) 495 3990

Iceland Tourist Board, 172 Tottenham Court Road, London W1P 9LG. (0171) 388 5599

Italian State Tourist Office, 1 Princess Street, London W1R 8AY. (0171) 408 1254

Netherlands Board of Tourism, 25-28 Buckingham Gate, London SW1E 6LD. (01891) 200277

New Zealand House, Haymarket, London SW1Y 4TQ. (0171) 973 0363

Norwegian Tourist Board, 5-11 Lower Regent Street, London SW1Y 4LR. (0171) 839 6255

Spanish National Tourist Board, 57/58 St James's Street, London SW1A 1LD. (0171) 499 1243

US Travel and Tourism, PO Box 1EN, London W1A 1EN. (0171) 439 7433

Washington State (and Boston/Massachusetts) First Public Relations, 2 Cinnamon Row, Plantation Wharf, York Place, London SW11 3TW.

PUBLICATIONS

Many publications are available from newsagents and bookshops. If they are free we say so.

AA/OS Walks and Tours, fifty scenic motoring tours and 194 leisurely walks through Britain - with OS maps and plastic pouch in a ringbinder which means a day's route can be taken out, there's no need to carry the complete book.

The Adventure Travel Book edited by Philip Pond and published by the Scout Association, Churchill Industrial Estate, Marlborough Road, Lancing, West Sussex BN15 8UG. Also available from this address is a series of free leaflets on buying 'Footwear' 'Rucsacs' and 'Sleeping Bags'. There are over 20 Camping and Outdoor Centres run by Scout Shops Ltd, see telephone directory for your nearest branch.

Alan Rogers Selected Camp Sites Guides, Deneway Guides and Travel Ltd, Chesil Lodge, West Bexington, Dorchester, Dorset DT2 9DG. (01308) 897 809

Best of British, free leaflet with details of the 18 or so top class Caravan Parks in this Association, PO Box 55, Exeter EX6 7YS.

Beanfeast - for free recipes using this soya based product contact Brooke Bond Foods Ltd, Leon House, High Street, Croydon CR9 1JQ.

Caravan and Camping Holidays in Humberside and *Walking in the Wolds*, free booklets from Humberside Tourism, Freepost, PO Box 80, Hull HU2 8QD or Tourism Hotline (01482) 211400

Michelin Tourist Guides. Separate books - Great Britain, Scotland, Ireland, The West Country and Channel Islands.

Perthshire Activity Line and *Perthshire Activity Days*, Perthshire Tourist Board, 22 Atholl Road, Pitlochry, Perthshire PH16 5BX. (01796) 474114

Quebec Adventure Unlimited, free booklet from Delegation generale du Quebec, 59 Pall Mall, London SW1Y 5JH.

RAC Outdoor Activities Guide, RAC Publishing, Croydon.

Scottish Borders, free holiday guide from Scottish Borders Tourist Board, 70 High Street, Selkirk, TD7 4DD. (01750) 20555

Staffordshire Moorland Activities Guide (free pamphlet). The Staffordshire Moorlands Tourist Office, 1 Market Place, Leek, Staffordshire ST13 5HH. (01538) 381000

UK Activity Holidays (comprehensive yearly guide), Charles Letts Ltd, Letts of London House, Parkgate Road, London SW11 4NS. (0171) 407 8891

SITE GUIDES

Most Tourist Boards issue free site leaflets. The following comprehensive guides are available at bookstores, newsagents, motoring organisations and/or from address given.

AA Camping and Caravanning in Britain and Ireland

AA Camping and Caravanning in Europe

AA, Fanum House, Basingstoke, Hampshire RG21 2EA.

Alan Rogers Camping and Caravanning - All Year Round - Britain and Europe

Alan Rogers Good Camps Guide (selected) - British Isles and Ireland

Alan Rogers Good Camps Guide (selected) - Europe

Alan Rogers Good Camps Guide (selected) - France

Deneway Guides and Travel Ltd, Chesil Lodge, West Bexington, Dorchester Dorset DT2 9DG. (01308) 897809

Benelux Nederland, Belgie, Luxemburg available from A van Zuthem, Haverweg 30,6991 BS Rheden, The Netherlands. 08309-51503

Cotswolds and Gloucestershire Caravan and Camping Guide Gloucestershire Tourism, County Planning Department, Shire Hall, Gloucester GL1 2TN. (01452) 425673

Forest Holidays, Caravan and Camping, Forestry Commission, 231 Corstorphine Road, Edinburgh EH12 7AT.

RAC Camping and Caravanning Guide Great Britain and Ireland, RAC Publishing, RAC House, Bartlett Street, South Croydon CR2 6XW.

Scotland Camping and Caravan Parks, Scottish Tourist Board, PO Box 705, Edinburgh EH4 3EU.

FERRY COMPANIES

B&I Line (0151) 227 3131

Brittany Ferries Tel: (01752) 269926

Caledonian MacBrayne (Scottish Islands) Tel: (01475) 33755

Color Line (0191) 296 1313

Hoverspeed/SeaCat (01304) 240241

North Sea Ferries (01482) 77177

Olau Line (01795) 666666

P&O European Ferries (01304) 203388

Red Funnel Ferries (Isle of Wight) (01703) 330333

Sally Line (0181) 858 1127

Scandinavian Seaways (01255) 240240

Smyril Line (Iceland) (01224) 572615

Stena Sealink Line (01233) 615915

Wightlink (01705) 827744

TENT MANUFACTURERS AND IMPORTERS

Blacks Outdoor Centres can be found in most large towns, see yellow pages or contact Blacks Camping and Leisure Ltd., Unit 3, Stephenson Industrial Estate, Washington, Tyne and Wear NE37 3HR

Cabanon: CGI Camping Ltd., PO Box 373, Newcastle, Staffordshire ST5 3TD

L Freeman and Son Ltd. (lightweight tents) 1 Bigg Market, Newcastle upon Tyne NE1 1UN Tel: (0191) 2321 646

I&M Steiner Ltd., (lightweight tents) Reynard Mills Trading Estate, Windmill Road, Brentford, Middx TW8 9LY

Lichfield: J.J. Hawley (Speciality Works) Ltd., Lichfield Road, Walsall, West Midlands WS4 2HX Tel: (01922) 25641

Marechal: SET International Ltd., Unit 2, Heathway Industrial Estate, Wantz Road, Dagenham, Essex RM10 8PS Tel: (0181) 984 8082

Raclet Ltd., 44 Birchington Road, Kilburn High Road, London NW6 4LJ Tel: (0171) 328 2167

Relum Ltd., Carlton Park Industrial Estate, Kelsale, Saxmundham IP17 2NL
Tel: (01728) 603271

Risol/Regatta, (lightweight tents) Risol House, Mercury Way, Urmston,
Manchester M31 2LT Tel: (0161) 747 5899

Sunncamp: Sunnflair Ltd., 46-52 Cutlers Road, Saltcoats Industrial Estate,
South Woodham Ferrers, Chelmsford CM3 5XJ

Trigano and Jamet: Tony Littler, 12 Ludovic Terrace, Wigan WN1 2QZ Tel:
(01942) 44598

READY-ERECTED TENT HOLIDAYS

Canvas Holidays Ltd., 12 Abbey Park Place, Dunfermline, Fife KY12 7PD
Tel: (01383) 644000

Eurocamp Travel Ltd., 28 Princess Street, Knutsford, Cheshire WA16 6BG
Tel: (01565) 626262

French Country Camping, 126 Hempstead Road, Kings Langley, Hertfordshire WD4 8AL Tel: (01923) 261311

Haven Europe, Northney Marina, Northney Road, Hayling Island, Hants
PO11 ONH Tel: (01705) 466111

Sunsites, Canute Court, Toft Road, Knutsford, Cheshire WA16 ONL tel:
(01565) 625533

SPECIAL INTEREST AND ACTIVITY HOLIDAYS TAKING
YOUR OWN TENT

Earnley Concourse, Earnley, Chichester, West Sussex PO20 7JL Tel: (01243)
670392 (special interests for over 16's, also residential)

New Forest Water Park (water sports with small camp site) Hucklesbrook
Lakes, Ringwood Road, Nr. Fordingbridge, Hants Tel: (01425) 656868

PGL Adventure Family Holidays, (also residential) Alton Court, Penyard
Lane, Ross-on-Wye, Herefordshire HR9 5NR

Sports Council (south west - golf tennis or bowls) Tel: (01202) 885970 or
(01460) 73491

Eurocamp Independent Ltd., 28 Princess Street, Knutsford, Cheshire WA16
6BN Tel: (01565) 625544

RESIDENTIAL ACTIVITY AND SPECIAL INTEREST HOLIDAYS

Headwater Holidays, 146 London Road, Northwich, Cheshire CW9 5HH
Tel: (01606) 48699 (walking, cycling and languages in France)

HF Holidays Ltd., Imperial House, Edgeware Road, Colindale, London
NW9 5AL Brochure line:(0181) 905 9388

High Trek Snowdonia, (option of night/s in tent) Tal y Waen, Deiniolen,
Gwynedd LL55 3NA Tel: (01286) 871232

Losehill Hall, Peak National Park Centre, Castleton, Derbyshire S30 2WB
Tel: (01433) 620373

Ramblers Holidays, Box 43, Welwyn Garden City, Hertfordshire AL8 6PQ
Tel: (01707) 331133 (mostly for over 16's)

YMCA National Centre, Lakeside, Ulverston, Cumbria LA12 8BD Tel:
(015395) 31758

WALKING GEAR MANUFACTURERS

Karrimor International Ltd., Petre Road, Clayton-le-Moors, Accrington,
Lancs BB5 5JP Tel: (01254) 385911

Merrell Footwear Ltd., CCS Centre, Vale Lane, Bedminster, Bristol BS3 5RU
Tel: (01179) 636 363

Mountain Equipment, Dawson Street, Hyde, Cheshire SK14 5EF Tel: (0161)
366 5020

Rohan Design plc, 30 Maryland Road, Tongwell, Milton Keynes MK15
8HN Tel: (01908) 618 888

MISCELLANEOUS ADDRESSES

Berlitz Publishing Company Ltd., Berlitz House, Peterley Road, Oxford
OX4 2TX

Boots Company PLC, Nottingham NG2 3AA

Camping and Outdoor Leisure Association (outdoor trade association)
Morritt House, 58 Station Approach, South Ruislip, Middx. HA4 6SA
Tel: (0181) 842 1111

"Camping" (magazine) Link House, Dingwall Avenue, Croydon CR9 2TA
Tel (0181) 686 2599

Camping Gaz, 9 Albert Street, Slough SL1 2BH Tel: (01753) 691707

Canada Campers Inc. 510-1212 31 Avenue N.E. Calgary, Alberta, Canada
T2E 7S8

"Caravan, Motorcaravan and Camping Mart" magazine, Aceville Publications Ltd., 97 High Street, Colchester, Essex CO1 1TH Tel: (01206) 540621

Elliot Products, (sailmakers and tent repairs) The Sail Loft, College Road, Chatham Historic Dockyard, Chatham, Kent Tel: (01634) 408160

Evenflo Uk, 19 Trafalgar Way, Bar Hill, Cambridge CB3 8SQ Tel: (01954) 789440

Field and Trek (Good gear Catalogue around £2) 3, Wates Way, Brentwood, Essex CM15 9TB Shops at Brentwood, Canterbury, Gloucester and Slough)

Grangers International Ltd., Grange Close, Clover Nook Industrial Park, Alfreton, Derbyshire DE55 4QT Tel: (01773) 521521

Kampgrounds of America, (KOA) PO Box 30558, Billings, 59114, Montanta U.S.A.

Motorail Tel: (0171) 409 3518

Koala Camper Rentals Pty. Ltd., 180 Great Eastern Highway, Belmont, Perth W.A. 6104 Australia

Mothercare, Cherry Tree Road, Watford, Herts WD2 5SH

Ordnance Survey, Romsey Road, Southampton, SO9 4DH Tel: (01703) 792682

Select Site Reservations, Travel House, Monmouth Road, Abergavenny, Gwent NP7 5HL Tel: (01873) 859876

Thetford (Porta Pottis) Ltd., Unit 6, Centrovell Industrial Estate, Caldwell Road, Nuneaton, Warwickshire CV11 4UD

Todds Mobile Leisure Ltd., (good range of camping equipment) Coote Lane, Lostock Hall, nr. Preston, Lancashire Tel: (01772) 35360

Touchwood Sports, (camping centre) 426 Abingdon Road, Oxford OX1 4XN Tel: (01865) 246551

Wayfarer Foods (food in a pouch) Amotherby, Malton, North Yorkshire YO17 OTQ Tel: (01653) 693971

YHA Adventure Shops, (lightweight tent and gear leaflets) Executive Office, 19, High Street, Staines TW18 4QX Tel: (01784) 458625

*   *   *

Text printed by St Edmundsbury Press, Bury St Edmunds, Suffolk